·

HUNG

·

A

Meditation

on the Measure

of

Black Men

in

America

· H U N G ·

Scott Poulson-Bryant

DOUBLEDAY

New York   London   Toronto   Sydney   Auckland

PUBLISHED BY DOUBLEDAY
a division of Random House, Inc.

DOUBLEDAY and the portrayal of an anchor with a
dolphin are registered trademarks of Random House, Inc.

Book design by Michael Collica

Library of Congress Cataloging-in-Publication Data

Poulson-Bryant, Scott.
Hung : a meditation on the measure of Black men in
America / Scott Poulson-Bryant.—1st ed.
p.   cm.
1. African American men—Social conditions.
2. African American men—Sexual behavior. 3. African
American men—Public opinion. 4. Masculinity—
United States. 5. Penis—Social aspects—United States.
6. Competition (Psychology) 7. United States—Race
relations. 8. African Americans in popular culture.
9. Public opinion—United States. I. Title.

E185.86.P667 2005
305.38'896073—dc22
2005043628
ISBN 0-385-51002-0

PRINTED IN THE UNITED STATES OF AMERICA

October 2005

First Edition

1 3 5 7 9 10 8 6 4 2

To two people whose help and patience
and friendship truly changed my world:

Albert Harmon
and
Ipeleng Aneb Kgositsile

With Love

"People hate those who make them feel their own inferiority."

—Earl of Chesterfield

"I'm what your sister and your mother's always thinking of /
They put my picture on the cover of the book of love . . ."

—"Big Black Man," *The Full Monty*

"I think that I know something about the American masculinity which most men of my generation do not know because
they have not been menaced by it in the way that I have
been."

—James Baldwin,
"The Black Boy Looks at the White Boy"

CONTENTS

First, I'd like to thank my editor, Clarence Haynes, for showing me the way. You helped a brotha see the light.

I'd also like to thank publisher Stephen Rubin and the rest of the Doubleday posse: Meredith McGinnis, Alison Rich, Brian Jones, and Samantha Dell'Olio.

I have to give a shout-out to Tanya McKinnon, the best agent in the world, for keeping my eyes on the prize.

To David Watkins: for keeping me laughing and thinking and remembering who I am. Your help has been immeasurable. Your friendship has been inspiring.

More shout-outs: to Smokey Fontaine, aka "Big Smoke," for friendship and love and brothahood whether times were sunny or tough; to Sha Shane Carabello, for dealing with my insanity and still keeping it real.

Andres McConnon, Princeton's Finest, the Estonian God of Toronto: this project couldn't have been done without your finesse, your energy, and your speedy way with an e-mail or photocopy. Big Ups to you and many thanks.

Adam Mansbach for reviving the writer in me.

To my friends, who revealed themselves to me with such gusto and aplomb, I thank you for sharing your feelings and ideas.

And to the Bryant family: your love and support keep me going; thank you for letting me know that home truly is where the heart is.

Prologue

Dear Emmett Till:

   The first time I heard of you, I don't think I was black yet. Let me explain. By "black" I don't mean racially speaking. *You* might call me "Negro" or "colored" because I am "African American" (as we've decided we want to be called these days), as in I have two African American parents who biologically created me and passed on the brown skin and brown eyes and full nose and all the other genetic traits that mark a person as African American. When I say that I wasn't yet "black" when I'd first heard of you, what I mean is that I was still the safe and sound kid who moved through the world not knowing that the color of my skin somehow marked me, in some people's eyes, as qualitatively "different." I knew soul food and Mahalia Jackson singing carols at Christmas. I knew straightening combs and Afro picks. And I thought that Martin Luther King, Jr., was a member of my family because virtually every relative I visited had a picture of him somewhere in their house. I *hadn't* yet, on the other hand, been followed around inside a department store, hovered over by the prying eyes of wary security guards and salespeople. I hadn't yet applied to any colleges, so I knew nothing of affirmative action and quotas and race-blind admissions. I couldn't drive so I'd never been stopped for a DWB (driving while black). I don't even think I'd yet heard the word "nigger" used without an emphasized *"please"* behind it.

But I can recall the first time I heard of you. I remember older relatives talking and someone mentioned "that boy" who had gotten killed a long time ago. "Lynched" was the word he'd used. There was something about the sound of "that boy" and the look on my relative's face when he said it that made me curious. Curious mostly because I was a boy, and hearing a word ascribed to me with such an odd and pained look on the face of the person saying it piqued my curiosity. This, I should tell you, occurred around the time that *Roots* was on TV. So in my mind, I always associate you with Alex Haley's *Roots*. I know, *Roots* took place in slavery days of the eighteenth and nineteenth centuries and you died in 1955, but I connect the two things in my mind because *Roots* was the beginning of my "blackness" in relation to so many other things in my life—first and foremost, "whiteness."

I can remember looking up your name in the card catalog at the library. I can remember my young brain trying to understand what had happened to you. And I can remember having nightmares about "that boy" who was killed a long time ago, terrifying nightmares of ropes and black male bodies swinging from them.

There were, Emmett, many times I tried to write about you. Once, in seventh grade, we had to do an oral report of something from history. I wanted to report on you but I couldn't. Mostly because of the nightmares. So I did my report about the gold rush. You've been a character in a couple of short stories I've written, and a couple of poems, back when I fancied myself a poet in my college days. But nothing ever really coalesced for me creatively around the idea of you. Perhaps you were too real an image, too real an idea in my imagination, borne to me as you were in my preadolescence when so many things scared me yet intrigued me enough to only attempt to be understood.

Now here I am, a grown man, almost twenty years older than the last year you saw, and you still creep into my mind. And as I write a book called *Hung,* about black male sexuality and the way it's all too often the site of so many issues that creep through the ever-evolving dynamics of this place we call America, there you are in the news again. It is believed that there were other men involved in your death. Men who can still be prosecuted for what they did to you. Because you acted like a man. There are many theories about what happened to you that day. But most of them come back to the fact that you were behaving like a man might behave: you whistled at a woman whom you found attractive. And unfortunately you were behaving the way a black man is expected to behave. Sexually aggressive. And toward a white woman! In the South! The racists got their revenge.

Times have changed since your death, Emmett. And yet they haven't. Black men aren't being lynched these days— or so we're told. But we are still at the center of this unspoken question that gets asked all the time. And often that question revolves around sexual behavior. They're still trying to figure us out. We're still trying to figure ourselves out.

Peace man,
Scott

Measuring Up

Allow me to introduce myself.

My name is Scott and I am a black man in America. I've never done hard time. I've never been arrested. I don't have any kids. I know I'm invisible to many, but I also know that I'm highly visible to more.

I've been told that I am a success story.

I like to think that I measure up.

I'm a suburban kid. I was educated at an Ivy League university that at the time was dubbed the "hot college" because everyone wanted to go there. I've had some success in the Manhattan media world, and don't they say that if you can make it in New York, New York, you can make it anywhere? I've even been a "first black"—I was, I've been told, the first black music journalist to have a national column in a major music magazine. I named *Vibe* magazine *Vibe,* and I've interviewed everyone from Michael Jackson (when I was a suburban twelve-year-old kid) to Prince (when he wasn't doing interviews) to Mike Tyson to Dennis Rodman. I've been a regular on a TV chat show. I've done *Charlie Rose* three times. I've been mentored by some of the best my field has to offer and I've mentored some successful folks in my field. It's been said that I foresaw the success of Puff Daddy before anyone else in the forward-looking world of New York journalism. I live in NYC in the summer and Miami's South Beach in the winter, because I want to and because I can. I've had successful relationships, and I love my parents and my parents love me.

Sure, I like to think that, in the grand American rat race that is life, I measure up.

But even with a laundry list of accomplishments that makes my résumé attractive, there are still days when I go to the gym and I get out of the shower and wrap my towel close around me, because I am a black man, and for a black man I just may not—in the swinging-dick sense of the words— "measure up."

That's because, you see, I'm what people call a grow-er and not a show-er. In other words, my soft hanging dick is not the monster of Mapplethorpean proportions that draws looks of wonder and awe. Of course many men are grow-ers rather than show-ers, but that doesn't mean I'm not still conscious of it. Partly because I'm a man—and men are concerned about those things—but also partly because I am a black man.

In other words, I should be hung like a horse. I should be the cock of the locker-room walk, singing and swinging and getting merry like every day is, for hung brothers, Christmas.

But I'm not. I guess I could spend the last few seconds of my shower doing my own fluff job, spanking little Scott into some semierect state that speaks more to the size of my actual sex-ready self. But would it be worth it? To let that towel fly free just in case I get some stares from the dudes lining the room, stepping into their own boxers and briefs and bikinis? Of course it would be worth it, because I am a black man and black men are hung like horses. I'm not. So what kind of black man am I?

But here's the thing. I don't want to measure up in the locker room. I don't want to be the stereotype. I don't want to be Mister Myth, because if I am, then I'm just a dick; the big dick in the locker room; the recipient of the real, live, guy-on-guy penis envy no one talks about; the guy white boys hate yet want to be; the brother other black dudes recognize as representative of their gender; the stone-cold stud with a dick of doom. I think of black-man dick and I think that once upon a time we were hung from trees for being, well, hung. The sexual beast, the loin-engorged predator, the big-dicked destroyer not just of pure pristine white women but also of white men's sense of themselves. That's where black men have found themselves, culturally speaking: hung. Strung up from trees; lynched to protect the demure pureness of white women; dissed to soothe the memory sin of slave-raping white masters; castrated to save the community from the sexual brutality black men trail behind them like a scent—the scent of the stereotypical boogeyman created by the fears of a nation. And I don't want anything to do with that ugly American history, the stereotypes that have been created to control me—do I?

Hell yeah, my inner ear tells me, I do. Fuck history. Let's be real here: Who doesn't want to have the biggest dick in the room?

Speaking of history, here's a flashback, my own first history lesson, if you will.

The place: Providence, Rhode Island. The time: spring 1986, my sophomore year in college.

I'm dancing at the RISD Tap Room, a smoky second-floor dive just down the hill from Brown University, a sorta rathskeller hangout for the artsy students who attend the Rhode Island School of Design and the local beer drinkers who love them. I'm dancing, like I said, a plastic cup of beer in my hand, a baseball cap on my head, wearing a cotton Oxford shirt and a pair of Levi's jeans. I'm sorta buzzed and I want a cigarette. I look around for a smoker because I hadn't yet reached that point where I was buying my own cigs; I was still arrogant enough to think that if I bummed all the butts I smoked, I wasn't *really* a smoker.

There's one, a white girl in a plain T-shirt with a bushy crown of brown curls, nodding her head to the synthesizer beat of Depeche Mode while she sits at a bruised-up little wooden table behind me and my crew. She smiles at me and holds open the soggy red-and-white box of Marlboros sitting on the table among the cups of beer. I take a cig. She flicks her Bic. I lean in to light the smoke. Before I can pull away, she says, "You are so cute." And I say, "Thanks," and start dancing again. By the time the next record starts, she's standing next to me, dancing next to me, sustaining eye contact with a vengeance.

We dance. We talk. We laugh. Her name is Kelly and she's from Michigan and she was a student in Providence but she's dropped out to work and "experience life." She asks me at one point, apropos of, it seems to me at the time, nothing, "What size shoe do you wear?" I look down at my Nikes, wondering where that question came from, and that's what I say to her: "Where does that question come from?" She shrugs and smiles and says, "I just noticed, that's all. Then again, you are a big guy." We dance some more. And drink some more beer. And laugh some more. By the time she's grinding against me, to a song that doesn't exactly require any sort of grinding, I'm beginning to see the light. This girl wants me. She wants me bad. Here I was, dancing and drinking in the RISD Tap Room, feeling cooler than cool, a Brown sophomore in Levi's and a button-down shirt, dancing with a white girl to the guitar strains of the Cure, and she wants to bed me. Not that I went out looking for it—which, when you're a well-raised young black man like me, is what you tell yourself when a white girl comes on to you.

When you're a well-raised young black man like me the voice in your inner ear sometimes sounds like your dad, your dad who grew up in the South in the forties and fifties, who knew what it was like to live life on the front lines of the constant battle for black male respect. When you're a well-raised young black man like me, you check yourself when a white girl's dangling the come-on, and you wonder what it is about you that made her seek you out. Are you just black enough to nab a white chick? Or are you, like she says, just a cute guy who likes to dance and smoke in the Tap Room because the Tap Room is the cool place to be?

Cut to Kelly's off-campus apartment, where we can hear her roommate watching late-night TV in the living room, laughing at a stand-up comic. We can hear her roommate because there is no door to Kelly's room, just some Indian-type fabric hanging across the doorway, blowing in the slight breeze from the open window near her bed.

We're done, me and Kelly. I'm a little new to this, this meeting a strange girl and going to her spot and getting some ass. I'm also new to sex with white girls. I didn't do it in high school and the only girl I'd fooled around with at Brown was a black chick who, I'd later find out, didn't really want to be with dudes anyway. But we're done, me and Kelly, and we're lying there, twisted in the sheets, sweating, postorgasmic, passing a cigarette between us like we're in some French New Wave movie.

She turns to me, reaches down, and touches my dick. And she smiles. "That was really good," she says. And then she says, "I thought you'd be bigger than you are."

I look down at myself, turn to her, and shake my head. "So did I."

Which was true.

"Why?" I ask her.

"Because you're black," she replied. "Black guys have big penises."

I didn't know what to say to that. Inside, I felt this sudden explosion of self-doubt. Partly because I'd had a cousin who'd explained to me when I was a kid that if you have a little dick, you're not a man. I knew I didn't have a little dick, but apparently I didn't measure up to expectations, for myself and this chick at least. So this is what happens when you fool around with white girls? Later a buddy of mine, upon hearing this story, says yes, it is, telling me, "You got White-Girl-ed."

Which in his mind meant I'd been dragged home with Kelly because I was black, because she was white, and because she was experiencing a little of what Spike Lee would soon popularize as Jungle Fever.

See, White-Girl-ed meant that I hadn't been out there trolling to bed a white chick. White-Girl-ed meant that I hadn't *had* to go out there trolling for a white chick. I didn't have to, my buddy explained, because there were enough of them out there trolling for us, for black men, for the big black dick of their fantasies, for the big black dick they had probably been warned their whole lives against seeking out. And why was that exactly? The flip side of fantasy, the other side of desire, was the distorted fun-house-mirror image of black men as objects of fear; the myth of the black man as the big-dicked beast, always on the lookout for vulnerable white girls and eager to purloin them of their purity, had been so culturally enforced that trolling for white girls was pointless: endowed with the enduring myth of sexual aggressor, demonized by it though we may be, black men only end up being more attractive to them.

"White people believe in myths," he said. "They have to, or else they couldn't exist. Nor could we," he added, "in their eyes, at least."

This was the beginning of an education for me, an education in the twisted ways in which race and sex rage through American culture, fanning the flames that are constantly charring the walls of America, the place James Baldwin called "this burning house of ours." Sure, I'd seen *Roots*. Sure, I knew my black history, all the names and dates and events that built the totems of black pride that defined my community and myself. I'd been educated in the ways of white folks, about the hurtling inevitability of racism rearing its ugly head, even in a world where some of my best friends were white. I'd even heard my father's words about dating white women, about the very real possibility of some white people (and some black people) taking issue with such behavior. I'd heard all that.

What I didn't have was any insight into the potential for self-discovery that occurs when all the discordant strands of lessons I'd learned were braided into one big cohesive lesson. Because it wasn't only Kelly's bold forthrightness that bothered me, her "white" way of making me feel "black" when all I was trying to be was a guy. I was also bothered by my response to what she'd said to me. For me, through all the lessons learned up to then, there had never been an intersection of race and sex before I'd lain down with the white chick in Providence. I'd risen from her bed a changed man.

"So did I." That had been my response to her statement. "So did I," as in: I agree, I thought I'd have a bigger dick, too. There was shame in that response but also a nagging question, as in: Why the shame? What had seeped into my consciousness about my emotional self that could be so affected by a quantitative judgment about my physical self? I partly knew the answer to that. The same cousin who'd told me about the lack of masculinity that came with a little dick had also once told me—when I was about thirteen—that eight and a half inches was average. And I *knew* I wasn't packing an eight-and-a-half-inch dick, and since I was probably about to stop growing, I never *would* be packing an eight-and-a-half-inch dick. I thought of myself as damaged and I was ashamed of it. Of course some of this also had to do with my thorough lack of sexual experience. I had no idea what women wanted and I had no idea whether I'd be able to satisfy them with whatever size dick I had. I'd had sex before but I was, essentially, an emotional virgin. And an idiot, truth be told, still carrying around my cousin's Guide to Sex in my teenaged brain.

I ultimately had to figure out that my cousin's lectures to me were all about us being guys. Black guys, yes, but guys nonetheless. Now I had my experience with Kelly and my college buddy's White-Girl-ed education to add a race element to that. What was it about my "guyness" that was truly supposed to be defined by my "blackness"?

More sex with Kelly didn't exactly answer all the questions I suddenly had—except one: that I wasn't the first black guy she'd slept with. More sex with Kelly did, however, change both my sexual and racial relationship to her. I knew now that I was a "black" guy having sex with a "white" woman. And there was something actually liberating about that. All the cards were on the table and there was nothing political or cultural to bluff through anymore. The well-raised young black guy in me didn't behave in such a well-raised way when we got together two more times. Somehow I'd figured out that even if I didn't have the huge black penis of her fantasy I could still fuck her like I did. We were louder, rougher, tougher, blacker. We never met each other's friends. We only screwed like animals in the room with the Indian-print cloth across the door. She thought I'd be bigger and so had I. But it was enough for both of us. Because, I suppose, at the end of the day, in the sweaty, postcoital silence poked through with cigarette puffs, we both sort of suspected about my dick what James Baldwin had written in *Just Above My Head*: "It was more a matter of its color than its size . . . its color was its size."

Ultimately, when the sex had run its course, when I'd gone my way and she'd gone hers—sexually satisfied on her part, a little mortified on mine—my sexual education was in full swing.

The discovery that I could be affected by someone else's devotion to culturally prescribed mythology; that I could actually want to maintain the myth, yet tug against the very pull of it; that I would have to live up to my own expectations as well as the misplaced expectations of others—this was my sexual revolution. It was everything I'd gone to college for. It was the beginning of my desire to want to understand "desire," to find the place where we transcended the usual stereotypes, yet carried them around with us like stowed luggage we knew we'd have to deal with but wouldn't have to look at during the whole trip. I'd been somebody's black buck before I knew that that's what she'd wanted me to be. Yet, just like she'd expected and just like I'd wanted to, I'd turned her out—she'd certainly come back for more. I could be ashamed of one of those roles, and still live to brag about the other to my friends.

Come to find out I wasn't the only brotha who'd experienced this—definitely not there at Brown, there in Providence—aptly named, looking back. *Providence,* as defined by *The American Heritage Dictionary*: "Care or preparation in advance; foresight."

My history lessons would be informed by the present-tense

discussions of life with my black brothers, other young black guys like me caught up in similar circumstances, trying to make history while we found ourselves caught up in American history's far- and long-reaching web. We shared the eternal conflict of "measuring up"—balancing the burden of the white stereotype with the complicated desire to maintain the myth, to grow up from the Bigger Thomas within, yet stay on speaking terms with the Dolomites we yearned to be.

Strange Fruit, or History Repeating

Depending on who you ask, the black man, as an American concept at least, was invented sometime around 1633, around the time—less than twenty years after the first Dutch ships brought Africans to pick tobacco and rice on the Southern plantations of the New World—that a Virginia court decided that any child born to a slave mother was also, alas, considered a slave. Or perhaps it was in 1750, when Georgia became the last of the British North American colonies to legalize slavery. Already considered a cultural savage, a religious heathen, and a social inferior, the black man (or the African) was now also a slave and, thus, an even more heightened version of those three prior roles. Within this new (but not newly) American construct of slave and master, this schematic of cultural and sexual and psychological rape, there would (and could only) result a redefinition of blackness: gradations of color, for instance, informed by the infusion of white blood into African bodies, meant a conflicted relaxation of some of those fixed notions of savagery, heathenry, and inferiority. The dialectic of "house nigger" versus "field nigger"; the Christianity forced upon the slave and ultimately shared with the master; the creation of a new class of colored folks discussed, debated, and defined in the ever-widening geographical schism that was the United States of America.

By the time the black man was able to attach the word "free" to the words that already described and defined him—let's say, officially speaking, in 1865 or so—he had already been so culturally entrenched as some objective "other," a creation of the collective imagination of white men who had as much of an economic reason to set him free as they had to keep him enslaved, that the act of existing, of living day-to-day, became the sole task of life. Who had time to reinvent himself when the mad scientists who had invented you in the first place would still find a way to keep you in your already culturally prescribed place? Not that the black man wouldn't try. He would have allies in his struggle, he would battle through indentured-farmer status and the lynching days of Jim Crow and the civil rights movement and Black Power, and every battle, whether the seeking of voting rights or good housing or education, would often be fought upon a mined landscape of masculinity. Which is not to shortchange or ignore the accomplishments and advancements made by black women in the struggle for race equality. But the very history of the United States of America, politically, economically, culturally, is built upon a continual reinvention of uses and misuses of the black body, and the black male body has too often been the site of galvanic battles and changes that have defined the very basic meanings of power relations and the shifting cultural codes and myths of American masculinity. There is probably no more powerful place of that misuse than in the hideous act of lynching.

I was educated by a photograph. This photograph showed

a Mississippi crowd gathered around a tree from which hung a young black man, a noose around his neck, his clothes bloody from the beating he took before the hanging. As shocked as I was by the sight of the hanging body, my eyes found it hard to leave the images of the placid, smiling faces of the onlookers, most of them gazing up at the body with a mixture of boredom and satisfaction, as if watching a movie they'd seen before yet enjoyed to no end.

Research cured me of the notion that lynchings took place at night, under cover of darkness, by Southern men with white hoods covering their faces. There were those lynchings, the sort of secretive abductions of black men whose lives were taken by being burned or beaten and eventually hanged. The knowledge, however, that lynchings—during the period of Jim Crow following the Civil War and the close of Reconstruction—were often advertised in the local newspaper as a community event turned my stomach. The literature I found about lynchings took pains to explain that blacks weren't the only victims. Southern whites who fancied themselves "real Americans" lynched Native Americans, Jews, Asian immigrants, and Latinos, anyone who challenged the sense of superiority that "real Americans" felt they possessed. Between 1882 and 1964, according to numbers in Leon F. Litwack's *Trouble in Mind: Black Southerners in the Age of Jim Crow,* approximately 2,017 blacks were lynched by mob-lynch law. According to Robert L. Zangrando in *The Reader's Companion to American History,* the number of recorded lynchings of black men and women between 1882 (when reliable numbers were first collected) and 1968 (when, he says,

the classic forms of lynching "disappeared") was 3,446. At
the crowded, advertised lynchings, attended by families like
some twisted church service or circus, body parts were sev-
ered and distributed as souvenirs. You could watch a lynching, have a nice drink and meal, and go home, if you were
lucky, with the fingers or toes or ears or genitalia of lynched
blacks as a memento of your night out. This was how social
order was restored. Mob-lynch law might punish someone for
stealing, for speaking out of turn to a white person, for just
being black. And there was often a sexual component to the
"crimes" for which black men were lynched, most often, the
crime of raping a white woman. But, it should be noted, just
looking at a white woman in the wrong way could also be
considered a crime, punishable by hanging.

According to Stephen J. Whitfield, in his study of the
Emmett Till case, *A Death in the Delta,* American culture in
the late nineteenth and early twentieth century was rife with
both official discussion and popular discourse on the notoriety of the "black savage" and his desire to conquer pristine
Southern white womanhood. Whether in the legislature,
which prohibited the cohabitation of the races, or in best-
selling novels like *The Clansman* (1905), in which a white
"mother and daughter commit suicide to escape the shame of
the daughter's rape by a black man," followed by a blood-
thirsty act of revenge by the white men in the town, the notion
of the rampaging black rapist became even more enforced.
Lynching, as an appropriate form of punishment, was even espoused by elected officials like "Pitchfork" Ben Tillman, a
South Carolina governor and eventual U.S. senator, who, ac-

cording to Whitfield, campaigned with the idea that he "would lead a mob to lynch the negro who ravishes a white woman."

This "sense of dread" regarding the black man and his savage pursuit of white women, his tendencies toward miscegenation that would only spoil Southern gentility and life, permeated the South in the years following the Civil War and Jim Crow. The lynching culture of the South succeeded at creating an atmosphere of fear for the black community and also spurred the rise of "legal lynching," as historian Jacquelyn Dowd Hall called it, a surrogate mob mentality that saw its bloodthirst carried out by courts that found black men guilty of crimes and eventually sentenced them to death. But that fear was also about teaching the black man where his "place" was in the social and cultural hierarchy, a precautionary move by the white power structure to maintain its superiority, its status over the negro, the prevailing culture of segregation. As Gunnar Myrdal found when he did his landmark study of Southern culture, *An American Dilemma: The Negro Problem and American Democracy,* white Southerners, when asked to choose from among six categories (what they believed blacks most wanted), first on their list was "intermarriage and sex intercourse with whites." Prominent segregationists often espoused the same ideas when asked about American culture's (and black's) fervent stride toward desegregation. Desegregation of schools, churches, and public space in general, was just a way for the black man to get closer to the white woman and sully the white race.

A friend of mine from the South once told me a story that he'd heard—I'm still not sure if it's true—about a crazy old white man who'd lived in his neighborhood in the seventies. According to town lore, this old white man would threaten black kids with "stringing them up" if they got too close to his yard while playing after school. The rumor was that this old man had a jar in his house that held a black man's penis, cut off during a lynching. My friend didn't recall how he'd heard the story, only that the story made the rounds every so often, a cruel reminder of the life his ancestors had lived as black folks in the South.

I thought the story reeked of Southern gothic melodrama, yet I also found it fascinating. I tried to write a short story in college called "The Memento," about two adult children of a recently dead old racist and the jar they found when going through their father's things after his death. There is a hand-written note attached to the jar and something at first unrec-ognizable floating inside of it. When the daughter reads the note, she realizes that the thing inside is in fact a penis and that her father had bequeathed it to her and her family. (I never finished the story, so I never showed it to my writing class. And don't ask me what I was trying to say with the tale.)

In Whitfield's book about Till, he cites scholar Carl Degler's assertion that because the United States was outside the tropics, "the South became the only slave society in the Western Hemisphere in which whites outnumbered blacks." Whites in the States, then, were "more free to develop an ide-ology that underscored their own superiority" to blacks. That that "superiority"—built around an ethos of sexual fear and control—resulted in the creation of a myth that managed to degrade black men and yet make them more fascinating. Did the white man know this, as he was inventing the American black man for subsequent generations? Would he have aimed for another way of protecting the myth of pure white woman-hood? It occurred to me, hearing about the black penis in the jar, and eventually learning what I did about lynching and miscegenation laws and the fight for segregation, that the white men who invented America weren't trying to create a monster to subjugate. They needed a monster against which to measure their own monstrous actions. And only the truly honest ones kept a memento around to do that.

The penis-size game is a man's game. Measuring, giving something importance by the very weight of its existence, gauging something's relevance by the dimensions of its measurements: that's a man's game, played on the fields where monuments mark time and create empires and symbolize power.

It is the metaphorical power of a penis's size that gives it the psychological weight men lug into relationships with women and with each other. Essentially, it is a signifier—of power, of prominence, of strength. So many men like to think that our primary attention to dick size is about impressing women (or not), about filling up that space women have (or not), about succeeding as a man in the reflective mirror of a woman's or partner's eyes. But it isn't. It's a measuring stick of self-worth, of capabilities and fallibilities, of winning and losing. Listen to the language we use. When is a guy described as the "swinging dick"? When he's the one with the most power. When is someone "busting balls"? When he's deliberately attempting to cut another man down to size, even playfully. When is someone being hit "below the belt"? When that person has taken the roughest possible blow he has coming.

Size—it's a male concern: Who has it, who doesn't have it. Who wants it and who needs it. Who looks and who doesn't (want to) look. Or, to bring it all home: Who's a man and who's not—or, at least, who's not as *much* of a man. It's the men's magazines that run articles about dick size—how to change it, what to do about it, if it matters—because for so many men, it's the very definition of who they are. And not only who they are, but *why* and *where* they are. "Anatomy," according to Sigmund Freud, that great thinker about penises and life, "is Destiny." Or, as some postmillennial Madison Avenue thinker put it: "Life's a cinch with an extra inch"—which is the tagline for an exuberant advertisement for Dockers khakis, highlighting the brand's "Individual Fit® Waistband" that "expands an extra inch." You tell me what they're really selling to the hearts and minds and egos of American men, hanging loose in their brand-new pants.

And for a lot of men, how you hang has a lot to do with whom you hang with, where you hang, and, sometimes, how long you hang once you get there. All of this tends to get played out in the work landscape, where the matrix of personal ambition intersects with an almost narcissistic phallic preoccupation with winning the game. Consider the term "overcompensation"—and I'm not talking the extra overtime coins in the check you bring home from the job. Got a Porsche? Maybe you're showing off that you're a player making moves, but you're probably overcompensating for a small dick. Muscle-bound body in the insurance-office cubicle with no bodybuilding contests on the horizon? Maybe you're a gym rat of the highest proportions, disciplined and devoted to crafting the best pecs on the beach, but you're probably over-compensating for a little dick. Your paycheck, your girl-friend's bust size, the predicted over/under on that game bet, your dick size: it's all potentially measurable. Men measure. Bigger is better, whether it's that Hummer you drool over, that raise at the end of the fiscal year, or that dangling piece of flesh between your legs. As one Armani-clad media exec-utive said to me at a dinner party in midtown Manhattan re-cently, "If you're a man, you want to prove to yourself and to the world that you measure up, that you're in the game. And it takes certain equipment to win the game you're trying to play."

"Like the game of life?" I asked him.

"That's the only game worth playing. As long as you're playing with the big boys."

This, by the way, from a black Harvard MBA, who, it's said, has a huge dick.

Look but Don't Touch

I've always been fascinated by the fact that the past tense of the verb "hang" that's used when talking about a lynching, is "hanged," whereas when you're talking, say, about art, you can use "hung" or "was hanging." And it's been interesting to me that when describing a rather largely endowed man, we say, "He's hung like a horse" rather than, say, "He hangs like a horse." Is it because horses don't "hang" in the slang sense of the word, so it would sound strange to the ear? I don't know. I suppose I could ask a linguist one day.

A female friend of mine once asked me why we even use a variation on the word "hang" to describe a dick. "Does it really 'hang'?" she asked me. "Doesn't it really sorta flop?"

"Some do," I told her. "Though it might depend on how much vertical hang there is."

"Vertical hang?" she asked.

"Vertical hang," I told her. "As in hangature," I added, using a word I'd learned from a friend of mine who, as a self-described "dick connoisseur," considered himself an expert on the subtle nuances of dick size. Hangature, he'd explained to me once, was the amount of ability a dick had to hang. Some dicks, he informed me—because, at the time, he'd seen more dicks than I had—didn't have much hangature when they were soft. They just sort of rested on the testes. This is what small dicks usually did, though some larger dicks, depending on how the testes were built, didn't have a whole lot of hangature either.

I remember asking him how he knew all this, how he'd amassed his expertise on the subtle nuances of dick size.

"I look," he told me, bluntly, I'd thought at the time. But then, you couldn't be much less *than* blunt when talking about the nuances of dick size. "Don't you?"

"Don't I what?" I said.

"Look."

I didn't respond at first.

"Of course you look," he said. "All men look. Anyone who says he doesn't is lying."

I eventually told him that I did, in fact, look, though I was too embarrassed to tell him why I'd started looking. The first time I looked at another guy who wasn't my father was in the tenth grade, in a gym class with guys who actually undressed completely when changing into their gym clothes. There was a guy, let's call him Terrence, who I'd known from around school and who was two grades ahead of me. Terrence was a good-looking guy, athletic and popular. He played lacrosse and basketball. He was smart and funny and friendly, even to an uncool underclassman like me. It might even be fair to admit here that I probably had some sort of crush on Terrence when I was in the tenth grade, the kind of crush that was less about sex and more about hero worship or adoration, as in: Wouldn't it be cool to hang out with Terrence? Terrence had a girlfriend, a beautiful senior whom we'll call Cherie. And one day, as I left the guidance office between classes, on my way to the library I walked around a dark corridor and found Terrence and Cherie clinched in a kiss. The sound of the door closing surprised them, and they jumped apart, not wanting to be caught in their clinch. In that moment of jumping away from Cherie, Terrence also tried to cover his crotch with his loose-leaf notebook. But not before I noticed the erect bulge there in his blue school sweats. Not that I was looking. But, considering the hugeness of it, it had been hard to look away. That was the first time I'd ever seen the bulge of another guy's hard dick in person.

Terrence smiled an embarrassed smile. Cherie giggled, as if to say, "Oh it's just him," and Terrence winked at me, as if to say, "You know how it is, bro," and shrugged, then turned back to Cherie. I continued on my way to the library, my mind still trying to wrap itself around the sight of Terrence's hard dick. In gym the next day, changing into my shorts to get ready for running around the track, I couldn't help stealing a glimpse at Terrence's naked body as he stood before his locker and stepped into a jockstrap. It was important, I seem to recall, to see what his dick looked like soft, not erect. It was important to see how much it grew to get to the size that it was outside the guidance office.

I think of those two moments with Terrence as the beginning of my manhood. Self-conscious as I was about my own slightly chubby (and very boyish) body at that time, looking at Terrence—the first guy I'd *looked* at, as opposed to just *saw*—completely naked was like a door opening into a whole new world. For one thing, I fully realized that guys in porn magazines weren't the only guys with very large penises. For another thing, as confused as the looking made me feel about my own sexuality, it also set in motion the very specific sort of male insecurity no one ever talks about yet almost every guy feels. And what is manhood if not a complete and embarrassing grasp of your own insecurities in the face of others?

Besides the locker room, porn was the only place to see another guy's dick. I remember watching porn videos at friends' houses when I was a teenager. And no matter how many comments were made about "tits" and "boobs," there was always at least one guy there who'd comment on the size or the stroke of the porn actor's dick. Which felt like a discovery. Granted it was in the safe porn-ogling situation that I found this out, but it was surprising to find dudes who admitted to looking at what other guys had. Other guys looked? I'd thought I was the only one.

I've since asked other dudes about looking, gay guys and straight guys and bi guys, black guys and white guys, and most of them admit to having looked, and to still looking, when they're in a situation to do so.

"You gotta see where you stand," one buddy of mine told me. He played high-school, college, and professional football and thus spent much more time in locker rooms than any average guy might. "You wanna see what some other cat is working with. Another guy's size matters because it's almost like the way you check out his wife, to see what kinda man he is."

That is true, I wanted to tell my friend. But what if you're just curious? I remember standing in the locker room of an NBA team and being stunned by the dick size of one particular power forward. I tried not to be obvious about checking out his package, but at the same time, watching him walk to his locker from the shower, swinging heavy behind a corner of the towel that he must have thought was covering him (or not), it was hard not to notice. The difficult part was trying to ask him questions about the player I'd been there to interview, while he sat there, looking up at me, drying off his chest, his huge dick hanging over the edge of his little bench. I had to tell myself that this was a guy who was used to being nude around a crowd of strangers. It was funny, though, to catch another sportswriter also trying hard to *not* look at the power forward's package. It was even funnier when he noticed me, looking at him looking. Eventually I started thinking of my pro locker-room interviews as some sort of twisted civic duty, because every time friends of mine—mainly gay guys and women—knew I was doing a sports story, I'd get asked for a dick report. Of course I'd have to explain that you don't *usually* get a chance to look even if you wanted to because the locker room feels like a workplace, crowded as it is with reporters and players and cameramen.

"Yeah," said my dick-connoisseur friend, "and they're probably all looking, too. You think any guy's gonna get a chance to see how he measures up against some pro athlete and not take it?"

Apparently so, because even as my football-playing buddy explained to me, "When you look at another guy, it's like setting a barometer for your own manhood. Size matters to guys. And if you got a big dick nobody can tell you anything. You. Are. The. Man. And you probably end up getting looked at more than you do looking."

By the time I was a senior in college, I felt like my sexual education was pretty complete. I'd had some varied partners, I'd experimented in that way that I thought most kids did when they fled suburbia and ended up on Ivy League campuses. I mean, I'd seen *Carnal Knowledge*.

But something happened senior year that made me rethink my relationship to my own penis as well as the role it played in the world around me. I know that sounds strange, but bear with me.

I should probably frame this story with another story, one that takes place in 1995 and 1996, somewhere in the middle of the rise toward those successful well-hung NYC days I referred to earlier. This was a time I sometimes think of as the Front-Row Time: fashion shows and after-parties; name-dropping and air-kissing and fun; weekly appearances on TV and by-invitation-only concerts. I was running with a crew of models, chilling at the in spots, sitting courtside at Chicago Bulls games when my agent calls to tell me that the deal for the sale of my first screenplay has been completed. It was that kind of time, when I could still be fashionably late to my life and know that it was going to be there waiting for me to arrive.

I'm sitting in Casa La Femme, one of those in spots, with a bunch of those models, swigging back shots of Patrón tequila, when this guy comes over to my table, plops himself down, and says to me, "So I hear you have a really big dick." That stops the swigging for a couple of seconds.

"Do I know you?" I say to this guy, this tall, slim white guy wearing an expensive suit, smiling an expensive smile, and pushing an expensive swath of haircut behind one ear.

"I know who *you* are," this guy says to me. "And I know you have a really huge dick."

How does one even begin to respond to that? I could go into how it's sort of thick but I wouldn't call it big in the length department. But I don't go into that. I'm looking around the restaurant thinking this has to be some kind of joke, some *Candid Camera* moment thrown at me by my friends at the table, enjoying tequila and Middle Eastern cuisine. But their faces are as blank as mine. Finally the guy smiles and says, "I know you're Scott Pulsing-Giant."

He introduces himself and I look closer at him, thinking, "Well, he must have gone to college with me." That's the only way he could know about that name.

"Did you go to Brown?" I ask him.

"My brother did," he says, and points to the table where a group of people sit, laughing like they're watching the funniest skit *Saturday Night Live* has ever done. And I recognize one of the guys, who sort of resembles the guy sitting next to me. His brother had been at school with me, during that period when I wrote for a revived campus magazine called *Midnight Hour,* the cutting-edge alternative magazine for hipster sophisticates, covering music and theater and films and, in my column, sex.

Somehow, in planning the revival of *Midnight Hour,* I'd been commissioned to write an article about penis size. I'd written for other campus publications, mainly raw first-person cultural reportage about urban life, bulletins from the mind of the sort of smart, wannabe-hip black boy who'd achieved some limited renown in the college writing community because I'd spent time at *The Village Voice* during a hiatus from Brown. I'd written about my sexually free period, seeking the mundane in the exotic, stabbing into the heart of my own insecurities and splattering confessional bloodstains across the page. And now here I was, conducting informal polls on campus, interviewing undergrads on the important issue of penis size. It was fun, talking sex with beautiful lacrosse players and lissome dancers, getting people to share their personal stories with a public hungry to hear the latest missives from the minds of their classmates.

The article came out in the premier issue of the new *Midnight Hour,* the cover featuring a huge photo of new indie-film stud Steven Soderbergh, who had given us an interview (quite a coup for the magazine). At the top of page twenty-one, under a small banner that read SEX, was my article entitled "The Big Phallacy." It was introduced with a note warning that the article was sexually explicit, and also that if the reader was interested in reading further, to "enjoy, but with a condom. Be safe!"

The first line of the article read as follows: "Every man has a penis in his life; most men, however, have two." I'd learned, somewhere along the way, to grab them up front; one thing every writer learns eventually — never bury the lead . . .

The article continues:

Let me clarify myself. The healthy male has a relationship with his penis: he washes it, dresses it, jerks it off, fucks with it, etc. That other penis (found on the body of a lover or roommate or father or brother or teammate) usually doesn't garner as much attention; glimpses may turn into stares, but that other penis rarely gets fondled (unless, of course, no one will find out and/or an even exchange is guaranteed).

I like penises. And penises like me, I think. Whenever I start to think about penises, I'm reminded of two stories from my youth and one from this summer.

What follows are three short scenes: one about the time I asked my father about erections; one in which I played dick peekaboo with a male friend at twelve years old and was asked to "be the boy" because my dick was bigger than his; and one about the first kiss I'd ever shared with a guy, during which I got an erection, described in the most purple prose I could conjure up at the time. The purplest: "Our first kiss sent my dick into the stratosphere. Tongues and lips just fell into place." Harlequin Romances, anyone? Suffice it to say, the guy I kissed in that story commented on the size of my erection and declared it off-limits to any orifice on his body.

Reading "The Big Phallacy" again years after its publication is like looking at a picture taken at some drunken party and thinking, "Do I really look like that when I'm drunk?" Only now I'm thinking, "Did I really write like that when I was that age?" I remember writing the article with my tongue planted very firmly in my cheek, yet also with a sense of purpose, a desire to shock, to convince myself that I could push the requisite buttons to make the world sit up and take notice. Which it did. The article has a real loud feel and sound to it, the sound of a young man shouting at the top of his lungs: "Look at me." I wrote:

So here I am, a college senior, with sex not a hidden mystery, but a pleasant indulgence. However, like most boys (and a lot of girls) I know, I still think about penises: the smell, touch, and sensation of those tubes of skin that cause fear in some people, make some feel absurdly powerful, make others feel absurdly weak, and cause so much anxiety in so many folks.

Which brings me to the real question:

Does penis size matter? . . . Penis size truly doesn't matter when the person knows what he's doing, right?

Wrong, several people right here at Brown informed me.

This was, mind you, Brown University in the late eighties. This was the campus of the Ivy League hookers scandal; the location of the cyanide-pill-in-the-event-of-war scandal; the New England university that had heard itself once called the "basement" of the Ivy League but was now considered the hot college, the cool, hip, exciting place to be, where smart crazy people did dumb crazy things.

Reading "The Big Phallacy" now, so many years later, is like a weird Dorian Gray moment in reverse, looking into a portrait and seeing—instead of a wrinkled old man—the youthful, fresh-faced, brassy soul of yourself. Yet it's also like a fun-house mirror, portraying every youthful indiscretion one has to offer.

"The Big Phallacy" wasn't the end of it, as it were. "The Big Phallacy" didn't just come out on a Tuesday and go away by the end of the weekend. It became a campus cause célèbre. Everyone, it seemed, had read the little article about dick size.

SEX

THE BIG PHALLACY

by Scott Poulson-Bryant

PLEASE NOTE: This article discusses sexual matters explicitly, and may not be in the interest of all readers. If you might be offended by such material, we urge you to turn to page 23. And, as an additional note, *Midnight Hour* hopes that everyone will enjoy this article, but with a condom. Be safe!

(names have been changed because some of you people are gossips.)

Every man has a penis in his life; most men, however, have two. Let me clarify myself. The healthy male has a relationship with his penis: he washes it, dresses it, jerks it off, fucks with it, etc. That other penis (found on the body of a lover or roommate or father or brother or teammate) usually doesn't garner as much attention; glimpses may turn into stares, but that other penis rarely gets fondled or scratched or bathed (unless, of course, no one will find out and/ or an even exchange is guaranteed).

I like penises. And penises like me, I think. Whenever I start to think about penises, I'm reminded of two episodes from my youth and one from this summer.

Episode #1:

One day when I was about nine, I asked my mother, a pleasant woman who's a counselor to young mothers and pregnant teens, why my penis was small and soft sometimes but bigger and harder at other times. This pleasant woman looked at me for a while before stumbling over her words. "Ask your father. He'll tell you." When Dad got home, I asked him the same question. It was a Sunday night and my parents

Episode #2:

Daniel was over to play sometime in the summer of my twelfth year. We went into the backyard and pulled down our shorts. "Okay, you be the boy," Daniel said, "because your dick is bigger." I'd never heard anyone my age comment on the penis size of someone our age; just of the older boys whose zippers hid huge bulges, that seemed odd to us, funny almost. Who'd want something that big on their body? It seemed awkward, heavy. Our twelve year-old minds seemed to forget that our bodies would grow too, in relation to our penises.

Episode #3

This summer, I met a man I'll call Ronny. Ronny is tall and relatively handsome. His friend was going out with my friend so we spent a good deal of time together at the Christopher St. piers, at clubs, doing all those gay-in-the-summertime-away-from-college-life thing . One night we went to a club. I danced with Ronny and he worked me down like I've rarely been worked down on a dance floor. I like a man who can dance, especially a banji one: a rough (but not too rough) streetwise man. Anyway, I fell in love, well, if not in love, in lust with him.

Our first kiss down on the piers sent my dick into the stratosphere. Rarely do I get hard during a first kiss, but this was not a normal first kiss. Tongues and lips just fell into place. I

backed away when I got hard; I didn't want Ronny to think I was a ho who just wanted to sex, no matter how safe the circumstances, and leave it at that. He did, however, feel my erection. And later he commented on the size of my dick. It seems he'd seen me adjusting myself after the kiss. "You're not fucking me," he said later. "You're too big." "No, I'm not," I said. "It won't hurt." "I think it will," he said. And that,

---

The little article about dick size—"The Big Phallacy"

And everyone, it seemed, had something to say about it. I remember going to class the day after it came out and being inundated by questions and comments and opinions. Considering I already had a reputation on campus for candor and spontaneity, the comments didn't always surprise me. There were a few "Not again, Scott's," due to my tendency to let it all hang out on the page. There were a few "Way to go, Scott's" from some of the other folks who vied with me for that candid and spontaneous reputation. But there were also some "How *could* you, Scott?'s" from some of the black dudes on campus who, I was told, felt like I'd placed too much of an emphasis on black male sexuality on a campus where we needed to be taken seriously as scholars and thinkers, followed by many laughing choruses of "I can't *believe* you wrote that, Scott's" from many black women on campus. I got more than enough "Can I see it, Scott?'s" from curiosity seekers across campus—black, white, and everything in between. I was stared at, pointed at, laughed at, jeered at—and I could handle it all. I was used to writing controversial pieces and used to the varying responses.

Until the *Brown Film Bulletin* hit the stands that weekend. The *Brown Film Bulletin* was a weekly listing of the films shown by the university film society, but it was more than that as well. People looked forward to it because the film bulletin, a two-sided photocopy of short blurbs and scribbles, also dedicated itself to lampooning whatever was in the news the week of its release—national, local, campus-wide. That week's issue was called the *Midnight Film Bulletin* and the main attraction was the current issue of *Midnight Hour* and an article called "The Really Really Big Phallacy" by Scott Pulsing-Giant.

Thus, my new name was born.

There was a "Handy-Dandy Chart of Penile Sizes (Where does your member fit?)," starting at a toothpick and ranging all the way up to Scott Pulsing-Giant—in between were a green bean, a hot dog, a cucumber, a baseball bat, a tent pole, and a telephone pole. The biggest pole on the list belonged to Scott Pulsing-Giant, which measured not just big but into the "stratosphere."

It was funny. For a while, anyway.

It was funny until someone said to me, "You know, Scott, they're only doing this because you're black."

That had never crossed my mind.

"If you'd been some white boy writing about dicks they'd just ignore it and move on, but you put it out there about brothers having big dicks and they'll have a field day with it."

Was that the case? I wondered. I thought back on the responses I'd gotten initially from black folks on campus. That was one of the weeks when most of the black folks didn't look me directly in the eye. I was used to that by this time. It appeared that I was always doing something to upset "the community," whether that meant coming out about my stabs at sexual experimentation or dancing at frat parties like I was dancing at the Paradise Garage or pushing the envelope with a short play about gay sex in a black fraternity. But now, in the wake of the film bulletin, some of the brothers who'd avoided me lest my freaky ways rub off onto their conservative coattails suddenly had my back, which was somewhat surprising. Some of the same dudes who had chastised me for writing the piece in the first place were now defending me in the wake of the bulletin's writers poking their tongues out at something that had had its own tongue planted discreetly but firmly into a cheek. Surprising *and* confusing: Were brothers actually defending my right to present the big black dick myth after being bothered by the fact that I'd done it in the first place? Had my "blackness" transcended my "freakiness"? And if so, what were their motives? I couldn't really take time to consider them, because in the heat of the moment I began to question myself, my own motives.

Had I just wanted to shock for shock's sake? And was this the result of said shocking behavior? Could I be angry at the film bulletin, which in its day had taken on more sacred cows than little old controversial me and lived to tell the tale? I didn't know how to feel, actually. That is, until it hit me, rereading my article in the corner of the Gate snack hall with a chicken salad sandwich congealing on the table before me: "The Big Phallacy" sounded like I was bragging.

I'd written:

Rarely do I get hard during a first kiss, but this kiss is not a normal first kiss. Tongues and lips just fell into place. I backed away when I got hard; I didn't want Ronny to think I was a ho who just wanted to have sex, no matter how safe the circumstances, and leave it at that . . . Later he commented on the size of my dick. It seems he'd seen me adjusting myself after the kiss. "You're not fucking me," he said later. "You're too big." "No, I'm not," I said. "It won't hurt." "I think it will," he said. And that, it seemed, was that.

I'd only told the truth. I'd told the story just as it had happened. And that was the problem. Or so a friend of mine, Renee, told me. She said, "You cannot go around talking about having a thick dick at a place like this and not expect some white boys to get a little jealous of that."

I tried to explain to her that I wasn't writing the story to brag—besides, there was so much more in the article about other people's experiences and other guys' size. Could this really be a racially motivated retaliation?

"They want to make you look like a fool," Renee said, "because you wrote an honest piece about something that obviously people are talking about."

But I was beginning to think I'd already made myself look like a fool. Had I gotten so caught up in my own zest for sharing that I hadn't realized how ridiculous it might seem to others that I was talking about my own thick dick, thick enough to scare off a potential lover? In my mind, that couldn't have been the case. *I* certainly didn't think of my dick as too thick or huge or anything, someone *else* did. Which was why I'd concluded the article the way I had: "I believe (based on my experience and others') that one's dick is only as big as someone's orifice is small. One man's log might be the same man's toothpick, depending on who's receiving it." Hadn't that been my experience with Kelly, the white chick from the Tap Room?

Perhaps, I told Renee, I was supposed to be as objective about the film bulletin as I was expecting people to be about my article.

Perhaps, she said. "But you put it out there, and you've learned a lesson. A black man's dick is something the whole world finds interesting, no matter how modest you fancy yourself being."

In the years since the writing of "The Big Phallacy," I have been in London and Paris and New Orleans and Minneapolis and Los Angeles and Chicago—and in all of those cities, someone has come up to me and called me Scott Pulsing-Giant.

For all my conflicted feelings about the article and the resultant immediate attention, I was never so inundated with offers for sex before—nor have I been since. If I had a bigger dick, perhaps I would have taken on comers of all races, religions, and genders. I would have indulged the fantasy of every white girl who winked at me and every white guy who brushed against me at parties. I would have become the slut of Brown and lived my life the exact opposite way of a friend of mine, a guy I'd interviewed for the article, a black dude with a ten-inch penis who was actually embarrassed by his largesse. (More about him later.) I was caught somewhere in the middle: too self-conscious to come up short, too proud to fulfill the myth I'd aided into becoming a campus-wide incident.

But perhaps it wasn't such a bad moniker to shoulder or reputation to wear.

Perhaps this was just the other side of the experience I'd had with Kelly. Back in sophomore year—younger, less experienced sexually, and less sophisticated "racially"—I'd been objectified by a white girl who'd based her expectations only on her own limited experience with black men. Back then, what I didn't give her in size I made up for in performance. I had, as my buddy told me you had to do, fucked her like I had a big black dick. Now, years later, I'd made myself the subject, for all intents and purposes inviting objectification. And being thought of as Scott Pulsing-Giant meant that it wouldn't be just about performance. It would be about showing and proving, about carrying that big stick and talking loudly with it. Sure, my toothpick might have been a log to that dude in my article, but would that be the case with everyone?

As for that guy in Casa La Femme, the expensive-looking cat who'd plopped down and asked to see my hugely big dick, he ended up being a friend and business partner. And the re-enforcer of a nickname I'll take to every college reunion I ever attend.

The Long and the Short of It

A friend of mine, who had notoriously described himself as "king" of his "crew" when it came to dick size (and sex), told me that, at almost nine inches, he was considered well hung, at least by the women he'd been with over the years. This friend, let's call him Rob, is a handsome guy, tall and thin and light-skinned with curly hair, a great athlete, Ivy League educated, successful in his career. When I told Rob that a hustler named Nico described another hustler with eight and a half inches as being "sorta hung," he laughed. Not because he thought it was funny but because I was surprised. "Of course, he said that. The hot number is ten, isn't it? Ten is the number dudes wanna have, so they can say, 'I got a ten-inch dick.' Which they think will turn a woman on. Ten is considered the big shit. Nobody got twelve inches, really, but brothas think if they had ten inches, they'd be the shit."

I know two guys with ten-inch dicks. One of them, let's call him Nate, also agrees that ten is the "hot number," the ultimate measurement of a man if he's even remotely into measuring himself. But, of course, Nate can think that because he does have ten inches, which, to Nate, makes him a better lover. "Having a big dick," Nate tells me, "is like driving a

BMW or some other luxury car. It's not just that it's impressive and desirable and people want it, but you can also do more with it, go more places, hit the curves better, you know?"

Simon, the other guy with a ten-inch dick, doesn't find such a metaphor for luxury in his genitals. Simon thinks of his ten-inch dick as a burden to be carried like some scar of shame. Simon is a smart guy, another Ivy grad, a track star at college who became a Wall Street star after college. Simon might be smart but he's also, in Nate's eyes, too smart for his own good, if "burden" is the word he uses to describe his dick.

"How can it be a burden?" Nate asks me when I tell him about Simon. "Who doesn't want a big dick? Any race, any religion, any dude anywhere wants a big dick. That nigga is buggin'."

Simon is from the suburbs of a major American city. His parents are both lawyers. His maternal grandfather was a dentist and his paternal grandfather was a college professor. When Simon was growing up in the suburbs, he suffered from what I like to call Solo Negro Syndrome, which usually afflicts only the most sequestered members of the black middle class, those who find themselves embedded either in certain lily-white enclaves of the suburbs or bused to such environs from their blacker surroundings. Simon had been the Solo Negro in his Cub Scout troop; he was the Solo Negro in his elementary-school class; he was the Solo Negro in most of the activities his parent's forced him to participate in, except for Jack and Jill, an insular club made up of the scions of America's black middle class.

When Simon talks, you can hear the cadences of a black boy raised among whites, the clipped italicized ends to declarative sentences that come out sounding like questions, an odd mixture of Locust Valley lockjaw and San Fernando Valley boy. When Simon talks about his upbringing, particularly his Solo Negro status in the suburbs, there's always a tinge of narrative distance in his words, as if he's telling the story of someone else's experience, as if any lingering memories he has of those days actually belong in someone else's head and heart. He manages to sound both proud and bitter to be such an embodiment of the post–civil rights American dream.

When I ask him about that mixture of pride and bitterness, Simon tells me about his cousins, the ones who didn't cross over into the suburbs, who lived in another major American city, in an apartment project that was nothing like the split-level ranch house Simon grew up in. He spent vacations with these cousins.

To his cousins, Simon tells me, he was bourgie, middle class, and thus not as black as they were. He was a "white boy." Which meant he was soft, a pussy, not as much of a man.

But that all changed one day.

"The only time my cousins in the projects gave me any respect," recalls Simon, "was when we all went swimming one summer and they saw my dick. I was the bourgie kid from the suburbs but I had the biggest dick of any of them."

Which meant? I asked him.

Which meant, Simon told me, "that after all that time they thought I wasn't as much a 'man' as they were. I was now *more* man than they were because I had this dick that theirs couldn't compare to."

But you were swimming, I said to him. How could anyone know yours was so much bigger than anyone else's?

Remember that thing about hangature? Well, Simon has major hangature. But that wasn't all.

"You ever heard of a circle jerk?" said Simon.

Never in the context of black boys, I said. I thought only white guys had circle jerks.

"This didn't start off as a circle jerk," he said. "It started off with us watching pornos on the VCR, me and my two cousins. One of them commented on seeing my dick when we'd changed at the pool. I didn't say anything. But there we are, fourteen years old, watching some big-titty chick in a porn film and we all got hard-ons and my cousin pulls out his dick and starts stroking it and then next thing you know we all are. And my cousin Sean didn't take his eyes off of my dick. After we were done, he said again that I had a big dick. I didn't even know what he was talking about. The only hard dicks I'd ever seen were in porn films, never one in person except my own, and I was always the same size if not bigger than the guys in porn films, so what did I know? And I definitely noticed two things from my cousin after that. He was really cool to me, never called me out for being bourgie, and he never ever introduced me to any girls after that. I think he was jealous of me."

That, I told him, didn't sound like reason enough for his dick to be a burden to him. That sounded like the sort of story a guy would be proud of, from all the talk I'd heard from dudes over the years.

"That was when I linked dick size to being a black man," said Simon. "I wasn't 'black enough' for my cousin until he saw what I was packing. Suddenly I was a real 'brotha,' you know what I mean? And," Simon added, "I started fucking soon after that and when you start fucking, you learn a lot more about the world."

It turns out that when Simon started fucking, he started fucking white girls, daughters of his parents' friends. "There wasn't anybody else to fuck around with," he told me. "Unless I wanted to do the girls in Jack and Jill, and I didn't because that would get back to my folks."

Ah, yes, I thought, the old white-girl-by-default school of virginity loss, if you're suffering from Solo Negro Syndrome.

"So," Simon continued, "this girl Laura told another girl about me and next thing I know this other girl is all over me, wanting some sex. We did it and eventually I fooled around with all the girls in their little clique. And that leads to the brother of one of these girls getting up in my face about me thinking I'm better than everyone else."

Did he mention sex? I asked.

"Not really, no. He just kept saying that I thought I was better than everyone, and that I didn't need to treat girls the way I was treating these girls, going through all of them. It was his friend, this other white kid, who jumps in and says it's 'cause I have this big dick that I think I can get away with that kind of behavior. And after that it becomes this joke, about me and my dick. And it made me feel like somehow they'd always wanted to bring it up, but only after I'd started fucking the girls did it come out in the open. That's where the burden I was talking about comes from. I didn't like being the black guy with the big dick. It's like I'm some kind of walking cliché."

After Simon tells me this story I stop myself from telling him that even I'd heard about his endowment, tales of which followed him right from high school through to the lush campus of his college. It turns out that I knew the gay brother of one of the white girls Simon had fooled around with in high school. I thought that telling Simon this might increase the burden of his cliché status, and I didn't want him to think that his status as a walking cliché, as a walking phallic symbol, extended beyond just desirous white girls and jealous white guys to the gay guys in his world. I also didn't want to make light of him, because I felt bad when he told me, "I don't even like locker rooms now and I think it's because of that whole experience. I would catch guys looking at me in the shower, staring sometimes. Not like they wanted to go down on me or anything like that, but just, like, they were interested and curious about me and my dick."

And all this time, I thought I'd had a weird relationship to being nude in a locker room, with my very unimpressive soft dick. As does my buddy Rob, whose soft dick, he says, swings *abnormally* smaller than it does in its erect state, and who doesn't want any guy seeing his dick and thinking he's small.

"There's a power that comes from having the biggest dick in the locker room," Rob says. " 'Cause guys look at each other and we think about that stuff. It might sound a little homoerotic but straight guys look at others, kinda like a judgment. But really, it's a competition, like everything else in men's lives. And you want to compete. Even if *you* know that you get huge when you're hard, a lot of dudes still feel insecure in the locker room. I do. I wouldn't want someone to call me out for having a little dick—'cause it's not like you can say to some dude, 'Yo, I *know* it looks small here but you gotta see it *hard*, bro.'"

And here's Simon, an athlete most of his academic life, in and out of locker rooms full of other nude men, hating locker rooms for the exact opposite reason.

New York Times writer Robert Lipsyte calls the locker room "the last bastion of male adolescent behavior. A place where men can indulge their basest adolescent urges." I've always thought that men spoke louder in locker rooms, voices ricocheting off the stone walls like darts, as if we needed our voices to somehow cover up the fact that we're all standing around naked after a game or practice or workout. It's the place where towels are snapped at bare asses like rapid-fire tongues licking at ice-cream cones, yet also the place where pregame confidence has to be bred into the insecure hearts of men who are not so far from being little boys eager to go outside and play. Depending on one's desire to find signs or symbols in the everyday, the locker room is ultimately both a simple place of male refuge and a complicated site of masculinity, rolled, like a dirty mound of wet towels, into one seething ball of Iron John issues.

In his locker room, rather than gloat in the attention, strutting his stuff around the aisles so everyone could get a look, Simon took to changing out of his clothes with a towel around him, and to this day never showers at the luxurious gym he uses near his Flatiron apartment.

"I'm just too self-conscious," he says. "I don't mind being

the star at work. I don't mind being the star on the court when I play ball. I don't mind being considered important or well known for anything I've done or accomplished or achieved. But being thought of as 'the black guy with the big dick' truly creeps me out. It might make me 'popular' but it doesn't make me better in bed. I don't think I was born with some special set of sex skills because of the size or the color of my dick. I don't like the idea that it makes other guys jealous, black or white. When they pay so much attention to it, it drives me crazy. It's like I'm on a slave block or something."

Slave block. He might refer to guys "black or white" being jealous of his endowment, and he may still carry conflicted feelings about his relationship to his cousins and the blacker-than-thou race games they played with him when they were kids, but Simon still used "slave block" to describe his feelings about being the biggest dick in the room. And that says to me that it's the stares of white men that get to him most. These are the stares from his coworkers, his peers, the men to whom he has to prove himself as a thoughtful intelligent professional, the men against whom he competes for professional glory every day. Simon, Wall Street whiz that he is, finds himself right in the crosshairs of Eldridge Cleaver's theory of white male–black male relations, the battle between the Omnipotent Administrator and the Supermasculine Menial.

According to Cleaver in *Soul on Ice,*

. . . the white man turned himself into the Omnipotent Administrator . . . And he turned the black man into the Supermasculine Menial and kicked him out into the fields. The white man wants to be the brain and he wants us to be the muscle, the body . . . And the mechanics of the myth demand that the Brain and Body, like east and west, must never meet—especially in competition on the same level.

As the Omnipotent Administrator, the white man holds all the power—intellectual, economic, societal—and leaves to the black man, the Supermasculine Menial whose only relationship to power is dictated *to* him, the more inferior pursuits, all at the behest and all within the realm of power dictated by the Omnipotent Administrator. Thus we have the age-old dialectic of master and slave, owner and field hand, buyer and bought.

This dialectic is of course resistant to any interpretation but the basest of American historicity, conjuring—from literature, from film—only the scarred and ugly cultural testaments to white-black relations. So we have the black man, the African, on the slave block, his body rummaged like an animal's for every possible trait of strength and solidity to ensure the base level of his relationship to anyone who would exist in his world: the owner who would breed and work him and the slave woman who would breed with him and work alongside him. He isn't asked to think. He isn't asked to develop beyond his station. And he is never completely immune from perhaps the ugliest of all the testaments, the eternal undertone of the black man as sexual terrorist, a transaction based on fear and control: He is hung like the proverbial horse. He is a rapist. He has no concept of love. He is a breeding machine.

Is Simon's slave-block analogy a remnant of some collective black-man unconscious? Do we all carry some of that with us? Is it the residue of generations of black men before him, helpless to their own abuse, powerless, made to feel complicit in their own definition, in their own prescribed inferiority? Is it anger or shame that Simon is feeling, centered on his perceived hypermasculinity?

Eldridge Cleaver writes:

The chip on the Supermasculine Menial's shoulder is the fact that he has been robbed of his mind. In an uncannily effective manner, the society in which he lives has assumed in its very structure that he, minus a mind, is the embodiment of Brute Power. The bias and reflex of the society are against the cultivation or even the functioning of his mind, and it is borne in upon him from all sides that the society is actually deaf, dumb and blind to his mind . . . The struggle of his life is for the emancipation of his mind, to receive recognition for the products of his mind, and official recognition of the fact that he has a mind.

That's Simon's chip: he feels as if the moment one of the guys sees his dick and attributes stereotype and myth and history to it, they never really think of him the same way again. Game over. He scores, but not really. His dick wins, but his brain loses. As hung as he is, he feels un-hung when it becomes the center of his definition as a man. His desire, in essence, is to not be desired. At least not for the thing that defines him in a way that he doesn't want to be defined.

On the other hand, Nate, the other guy I know who hangs

ten inches, has absolutely no concept of what Simon describes. "Ain't no shame in my game," he tells me. A music-business professional, proudly and loudly a hip-hop head who considers himself an around-the-way intellectual, Nate is a guy for whom *The Godfather* refers as much to a cinema masterpiece as it does to a Spoonie Gee cut. Simon's relationship to the burden of the big black dick myth is, to Nate, confusing at best and dishonest at worst. For Nate, the issue of dick size *is* all about confidence, directly connected to his measure as a man, and definitely a measure of himself as a black man. As far as Nate's concerned, perhaps Simon has too much of the Omnipotent Administrator in him, and not enough of the Supermasculine Menial.

He told me, "Brothers use the myth of dick size as some power shit. We completely buy into it. When you're a black man, you know that a very large part of your identity is connected to the myth of your sexual identity, and people thinking we have huge dicks is how we measure ourselves, especially against white men. The idea of the big black dick might have started with white folks' myths but we've bought right into it. I don't even know if black men are necessarily bigger than anybody else, and neither do white men. They're just going by some crazy-hung African brothas they saw back in the day and applied to all of us because they could. But you won't get a lot of brothers to admit that we aren't all bigger 'cause we don't wanna wear that hat. There's just the assumption that we have bigger dicks and thus we're more masculine . . . We've bought right into it."

And do we have any other choice? For all of Simon's tortured experiences, is there the chance that we concede power back to whoever has it if we don't make the myth work for us? Do we forfeit strength if we admit to disowning the Supermasculine Menial role and aspire to more Omnipotence? Do we gain true power if we clutch the supermasculine as a cultural ideal which differentiates us from white dudes? We are Americans after all, with all the complicated, misplaced braggadocio that goes along with that. If one buys Nate's stance, does the black man's complicity in this myth mean that we get to negotiate shared control of our genitals and what they mean and have meant, symbolically, throughout history? Can we say the white man is jealous if we proudly let his myth define us?

"Face it," says Nate. "Black men are just the way so many men think women want their men to be . . . If you want the real deal about dick size and all that you should speak to some sistas. They'll tell you how it is. And I know what they'll tell you. They'll say it's all about the way a dude rolls up on them. Some sistas want brothas to have that image, you know, the big-dick stud. They support that like it's some Million Man March shit and they gotta be down for the brothas' cause."

So what about the other side of the coin?

A buddy of mine met a woman online and they made a date to meet up. My buddy, let's call him Dylan, hadn't had a date in a very long time and the sister he met on match.com seemed like just what he needed. She described herself as "plain but sexy," which sounded good to him since he thought of himself as an "average Joe." And, as he told me once on a flight to L.A. during which we confessed some of our deepest sexual secrets, he was "very very average, if you get my drift."

Let's call the woman he's meeting Lisa. Lisa showed up for the date after they had exchanged seven e-mails and had three telephone conversations. And she wasn't plain. She was, however, extremely sexy. "That picture I sent you is my 'maybe' picture," she told Dylan. "I send that when I'm not completely sure how far I'm gonna wanna go with a guy I meet."

They both worked in Manhattan, so they decided to have a "Brooklyn date" for a change of pace. A walk through the park led to dinner at a restaurant on DeKalb Avenue which led to coffee at a spot on Myrtle, which led to the two of them retiring to Dylan's apartment on South Oxford Street.

Retiring to Dylan's apartment meant making coffee and watching a DVD of *The Sopranos*—they both loved the episode where Carmela sorta threatened her next-door neighbor's sister into writing a college recommendation for Meadow. "We have so much in common," Dylan told me.

Watching *The Sopranos* led to some kissing on the couch. Which led to some groping. Which led to nervousness for Dylan. Because of his "very very average" description, if you get my drift. This was a precarious moment for Dylan. As he'd told me on the plane that day, making out with a woman for the first time always caused him a moment of panic because he was never sure how she might react to his endowment, "or lack thereof." Dylan had been in clinches that stopped abruptly when a sister reached down and found that he wasn't exactly packing major wood. Three clinches to be exact.

"Have you only been with three women?" I asked him.

"Hell no," he responded. "I get mines."

"Then what's the big deal?"

"You ever been rejected because of the size of your dick?"

I told him about Kelly when I was in college. Not a rejection but definitely a question asked.

That, to Dylan, was different. Kelly hadn't turned me down, she'd merely made an observation. Dylan, on the other hand, had seen women's faces change when they didn't find in his boxer shorts what they were expecting to find. "I'm six three," he told me. "I weigh two hundred pounds. You can see I'm a big dude. Except for down there."

And down there, we both agreed, was where it counted.

Or was it?

Down there was where it mattered to those three women. "You can't let that get to you," I said. But I knew my sensitive-brother words weren't getting to him. How could they? Dylan was a brother. He knew what the world thought of him, expected of him.

Lisa didn't reject him, as it turns out. They dated for a few months and broke up not because of Dylan's size but because Lisa moved to Seattle and wasn't into a long-distance relationship.

"Now I have to go through it again," Dylan told me. "Story of my life."

That doubt about himself stayed with him, the same way Kelly's words never completely left my brain.

I asked a woman friend of mine, a short, cocoa brown, beautiful sister named Patty, whether size matters.

Patty and I talk sex quite frequently. Probably because she

has so much sex and so little shame. Patty was the first woman I ever heard use the term "blow job" in reference to something she liked to do. She's also the woman who explained to me the finer points of the girth versus length debate when it comes to penis size, how all things being equal — money, job, looks, body, breath — thickness trumps length any day. And Patty knows from dick size. She slept with a rather well-known music mogul before he achieved his moguldom and she slept with him again after his moguldom had made him a media darling. His dick, she informed me one day over brunch in the East Village, had actually gotten bigger between sessions.

"Impossible," I said, nearly spitting out my coffee.

With a smile she informed me that maybe he hadn't actually gotten bigger. Maybe his newfound fame had given him a newfound confidence and he only screwed her like it was bigger than the last time. "Either that or he had some surgery down there. All I know is that he felt bigger than before."

So, Patty, does size matter?

"Only," she said, "if a guy has no idea what he's doing. And there are more guys like that than there are guys with little dicks. At least that's been my experience. And I've had a *lot* of experience."

I tell her what Nate said about sisters wanting to perpetuate the myth of black men having big dicks. She laughed. "Enough sisters, hell, enough women of *any* race, will tell you that a man who can work his fingers and his tongue will trump some big-dick dude any day."

I've been thinking of introducing Patty to Dylan.

"Just listen to what the sisters rhyme about," says another friend, Lena. Lena is a model and, as they say, she keeps it real. Not the most politically correct person, Lena tells you exactly what's on her mind, and I love her for it. Her ideas are her own and she believes them, no matter how wild some of her theories can be, with all her heart and soul. Race and sex are two of her favorite topics.

"You tell *me* if sisters are as guilty as black men about the big-dick thing." And she reels off some songs for me: "Trina's 'Big Ole Dick,' Missy's 'Work It.' And what about Lil' Kim? 'I used to be scared of the dick.' You think she's talking about some brotha with a *four-inch* dick? Hell no. Who scared of a four-inch dick? That wouldn't even hurt if she took it in her ass. Ya think?"

Uh, I guess not? But, I ask her, why would black women want to be complicit in propelling the myth of the big black dick? Is it just a way to prop brothers up? An ego boost?

Lena shakes her head of dreadlocks vigorously, then abruptly starts to nod, as if a new idea has flashed into her brain. "See, I think it's like this. When you're a black woman, you can't walk down the street without gettin' it from all sides. Brothas be after you, the Latin brothas be after you, the white boys really be after you even though they wanna act like they aren't half the time, 'cause they all think black women got some magic between they legs. Like black women will wrap you up and just make passionate love to you like nobody's business. And sometimes that's true."

"And another stereotype," I tell her.

"Sure it's a stereotype, the wild-chile black woman just can't get enough. But see, black women don't threaten white men like black men do."

"And?"

"So if the whole world thinks black men got these huge dicks swinging, that's power. White men get jealous over that. Surest way to piss off a white dude is make him think he ain't laying it on you like a black man would. And I think black women basically ain't mad at puttin' it out there that brothas got it goin' on below the belt. You can have all the power in the world, but if you can't satisfy a woman you won't feel like it. That's just real for men whatever race they are."

Talking to Lena made me think of a story I'd heard from two different people, once when I first moved to New York after college and again recently when I told some friends I was thinking of writing something about black men and the dick myth.

It's a story about a major Hollywood actor, a white guy, who's been known to ask his black sex partners if he's as good in bed as their black lovers. He asks in more blunt and scatological words, from what I've been told, and always demands an answer. Reportedly, he isn't necessarily offended if his partner tells him that he isn't as good as a black man. He thinks of that as a challenge, a reason to work harder, longer, stronger, better.

Talk about penis envy.

Green with Envy

I don't know what the fuss is about. I mean, everything in the world love you. White men love you. They spend so much time worrying about your penis they forget their own. The only thing they want to do is cut off a nigger's privates. And if that ain't love and respect I don't know what is. And white women? They chase you all to every corner of the Earth, feel for you under every bed. I knew a white woman wouldn't leave the house after 6 o'clock for fear one of you would snatch her. Now ain't that love? They think rape soon's they see you, and if they don't get the rape they looking for, they scream it anyway just so the search won't be in vain. Colored women worry themselves into bad health just trying to hang on to your cuffs. Even little children—white and black, boys and girls—spend all their childhood eating their hearts out 'cause they think you don't love them. And if that ain't enough, you love yourselves. Nothing in this world love a black man more than another black man. You hear of solitary white men, but niggers? Can't stay away from one another a whole day. So. It looks to me like you the envy of the world.

Those are the mockingly ironic words of a character named Sula, created by Toni Morrison for a novel named for that character, an angry and rebellious woman who returns to the small town which had raised her, yet had lost her, letting her slip through the gaping cracks of hypocrisy that lined its edges. Sula is speaking to a character named Jude, who has just commented, after a long day of work, about the burdens carried by black men as they travel the weary road to survival. A survivor herself, Sula laces into him with that speech. Decisively irreverent yet undeniably cunning in its offhand smarts, it only hints at the wily way Morrison has of transforming the traditional narratives to fit alternative visions of black life in America. It should be pointed out that the speech actually begins "Sula was smiling," and ends with Jude and his wife, Nel, laughing along with her, and it should also be pointed out that the speech is a sort of intoxicating seduction. Locating for Jude the source of all that "love" that comes a black man's way, Sula zones right in on his "privates," her laundry list of "loves" stopping only at the declaration of "envy," aligning love and envy into what is essentially a definition of "desire."

Desire and envy.

I'm reminded of a funny scene from Barry Levinson's 1999 film *Liberty Heights,* in which two eighth-grade white boys tell their friend, a precocious and curious white Jewish kid, that he cannot *possibly* have a crush on the beautiful black girl in their class—and if he does, he shouldn't *possibly* expect to get anything sexual going with her. And why not? Not because it's the early sixties and the Negro's civil rights is a new and challenging part of American life, shifting political and business loyalties in their own town. And not because miscegenation might still be considered a crime in early-sixties Baltimore. No. Ben Kurtzman is told to stay away from the black girl because, sexually, she'd probably only been with black guys—and hadn't Ben seen the dick on that black guy in the locker room? He was hung like crazy—one of the kids even used the thick end of a climbing rope to illustrate his description. Ben, being white, would *never* be able to compete with *that*. Mere preteen-agers and they were already limiting the parameters of their own desire by gauging themselves against the genitals of a black kid in gym class, declaring themselves losers in the sex race that the black kid doesn't even know he's running.

Yes. Talk about penis envy.

Which, it has been argued, is Sula's problem. She's mad that she hasn't got a dick, as a friend of mine argued back at Brown. Which, my friend theorizes, explains Sula's speech to Jude. According to my friend, that speech was Sula's way of saying that Jude shouldn't worry about whatever problems may pave the tentative steps of a black man's march to glory, because he may be black but he's still a man—and a man's got a dick, so that puts him at the front of the line anyway. I can't say that my buddy's Freudian reading of *Sula* convinced me, but his basing his interpretation of the scene on the theoretical analysis of the phallic stage of Freud's psychosexual stages of development—in which Freud theorized that girls discovered, around age four, that they lacked a penis, blaming their mother for this "lack" and thus switching their love affections onto their father—is one bold maneuver. Yet, frankly, it's too male in its reading. Sula may have wanted *some* dick, but she didn't want *a* dick. She was just, to use hip-hop parlance, keeping it real. Sula knew the deal; she'd borne witness to the complicated and complicit relationship between race and sex that informed her ironic position. The thin line between love and hate was a high-wire over the hearts and egos of black men that white folks walked with their eyes closed. Which wasn't exactly an ideal situation but it would have to do—as long as the black man, the desired, objectified, obsessed-over black man, kept *his* eyes wide open.

I wish I'd known a Sula when I was following Kelly home from the RISD Tap Room that night.

About a year ago, I read a letter in "Savage Love," the funny and popular sex column by writer Dan Savage, from a young woman who, after a long and fulfilling sexual relationship with her boyfriend, shoved a vibrator up his ass—at his request. This didn't bother her as much as the fact that, just before his orgasm, her boyfriend began to mutter and moan about being fucked up the ass by a big black man. This didn't bother her at first, either—fantasies and sex talk, after all, being, well, fantasies and sex talk. However, she began to worry more when her boyfriend began to tease *her* about wanting a big black man instead of him. What she couldn't comprehend, and the reason she was writing to Savage, was what this all meant: Was her man suffering from some kind of "penis envy"? Was he really into a "big black man" and merely projecting his desires onto her? Did she, in fact, need to worry about this behavior? Basically, Dan Savage told Freaked Out Female (her nom de plume): Yes. She needs to worry. Work this out now or expect to find your boyfriend creeping away in the night, looking for that "big black man" to ream his tight little butt.

Such, it seems, is the power of the "big black man" myth. It's not your father's racial stereotype anymore. It's not just for women. It's not just for white guys who want to fantasize about their woman taking it. Even "straight" white guys want in on it and are finally finding a language to express their desire for the big black dick. No one ever seems to fantasize about an average black dick. No one ever seems to fantasize about a big *white* dick. It's gotta be big—can you supersize that order, please? And it's gotta be black— *"I wanna see it,"* to quote the Rolling Stones, who built a career out of appropriating the swaggering slur and poses of old-school black blues, *"painted black, black as night, black as coal . . ."*

What exactly is the allure? What's the fascination? What need does it fill that the color of these fantasies is black, that the size is extra-large?

The letter to Dan Savage intrigued me. Not only did I ask myself all of the above questions but I was fascinated by the sexual switcheroo at work in the later sentences. The boyfriend enjoyed the dildo in his rear and felt the need to cast his partner as a "big black man" as she pleasured him, but the need to share the fantasy, to impose his own desire for the big black man onto his girl, struck me most. The simultaneous need to cast her as a big black man while using a dildo on him and yet maintain that she might pine for the same thing seemed to be an extension of the white need to cast the black man as supreme sexual aggressor.

But with a twist. In addition to being a mask to shield his own sense of sexual inferiority, it also seemed to be a way to mask what he might think of as his own sexual transgression. Recasting the act, the desire itself, using race as the site of sexual behavior, played down its "difference," made it somehow easier to indulge, or, as Macy Gray put it, "fly his freak-flag high." It reminds me of the name given to white gay guys who indulge their interest in—if not fetishes for—black men: dinge queen, "dinge" being short for "dingy," which in and of itself is a synonym for "dirty." The desire to transgress the norm, to admit attraction to something other than the all-American standard of beauty and attractiveness, is recast as the desire for something dirty or unclean. Not to presume that every white person with a taste for black partners indulges this point of view, but the constant deification of blackness as an emblem of sexual recklessness and abandon, not to mention size, never fails to amaze me. Which reminds me of a story my friend Danny told me about a night he spent at a sex party.

Danny's gay. He's a handsome, solidly built, light-brown-skinned dude. And he's a top. In other words, Danny does the screwing and rarely gets screwed. And though he will, at times, shuck the top label and declare himself versatile, Danny likes guys who consider themselves bottoms, guys who get screwed and rarely do the screwing. Danny also doesn't believe in boyfriends, not at this point in his young and successful life. Boyfriends only weigh you down, and besides, as far as Danny's concerned, no one person can ever really fulfill your every need.

So Danny finds himself at these private by-invitation-only sex parties, orgasmic smorgasbords in the finest penthouses in Manhattan, each one ripe with possibility, fresh with promise.

At this one in particular, however, Danny wasn't feeling his usually ebullient self. There was an appetizing-looking ass reclined across the leather sofa. Near the Warhol painting, there was an inviting-looking dick that was calling his name. Only thing was, Danny couldn't really get it up. He was as horny as a groupie at the back door of Madison Square Garden after a Knicks victory, but try as he might, he couldn't quite manage more than half-mast. He wanted to salute all the glorious action going on around him but his flag just wasn't trying to fly all that high. And erections weren't a problem for Danny. Erections, like most things, came easy for Danny.

But not this time, and he thought he knew why. Danny had just begun taking some medication which, erection-wise, took some of the air out of his sails, so to speak. He thought, checking out his limp penis in the mirror, that maybe he might lose *some* stiffness but *this* was ridiculous. This was criminal. Particularly with that appetizing-looking ass spread-eagled on that leather couch.

So he stood there, wallflowering it, watching the action, hoping no one would notice that the usual life of the party was in strict voyeur mode. Until the host climbed down from the leather harness swing in the middle of the room and sauntered over in Danny's direction. He said hello and reached down to shake Danny's dick hello. He wanted to know why Danny was sticking by the sidelines. Danny didn't know what to say. He didn't want to say the wrong thing and he didn't want his meaning to be misconstrued, so he just shook his head and mumbled something about waiting for the mood to hit him.

The mood.

The host tried to help the mood. He didn't want the mood to hit, he wanted the mood to knock a grand slam out of the park. And Danny knew it. It had been his excellent attention to this host on other occasions that had resulted in Danny's getting on the A-list. And Danny, a fan of art, wasn't mad at getting his nut off in apartments with living rooms that could pass for a wing of the Museum of Modern Art. So there he stood, looking at the host, who was looking at Danny's dick. The host was having some success down there, his mouth trying to work its usual magic; Danny felt himself stirring to attention. But it wasn't giving the room the kind of attention Danny liked to give it. So he hugged the host and began to walk away, to find his clothes, dress, and go.

"And where are you going?" said the host.

"I'm obviously not up to this tonight," said Danny.

"Of course you are," the host replied. Then he called over a divorce attorney who was there relieving stress from his own divorce proceedings. The host put the attorney's hands on Danny's dick and said, "Danny's trying to leave us. Convince him to stay."

The attorney dropped to his knees and started to convince Danny to stay.

Danny let him do some more convincing, then watched as the host dropped to his knees as well, to add his own two cents to all this convincing.

"But it's not getting hard," Danny said, finally.

The attorney looked at the host. The host looked at Danny.

"Hard?" said the host. "Who cares if it's hard or not. It's big, it's black, and it's uncut." He did a little more convincing, then he looked up again. "It's perfect."

"How did you feel when he said that," I asked Danny later that night on the phone.

"How do you think I felt?" said Danny. "My dick was in his mouth."

"But you didn't get a nut," I said.

"I did when I got home," said Danny.

"But how did you feel at the party?"

"I got invited back," he said. "So tell me what I missed on the game. Did the Knicks win?"

So. Danny's dick was perfect. It wasn't even hard and it was the life of the party. *The color* was *its size. The size* was *its color.* And here's the thing: Danny doesn't even think he has a big dick. It's "nice," he says, but not monstrously big. Nonetheless, this is the reaction he gets from his primarily white sex partners. Great for his ego, and great for a laugh, sometimes.

"What's funny," Danny tells me, "is that the size queen in me always thinks, 'What are they going on about? I have bigger dildos than this at home.' I mean, I like a big dick as much as the next person. I want to be impressed by it, too."

Lately, though, Danny has been thinking about what this all means, this status of his, about his own desire to be desired in these situations. His feelings are conflicted. One goes to a sex party to be eroticized, but what happens when that eroticization feels like exoticization?

"There are times," he tells me, "when I feel almost disconnected from it, like I'm not part of it. Or like the desire for my dick allows the rest of me to not be a part of the situation. It's a sex party, so you can't really take it that seriously, and resisting it would mean, on some level, resisting the reasons for being there, which are to leave everything else at the door, get a nut, have fun, leave."

Yet he acknowledges that although he enjoys the experience, it can be hard to feel attractive in a setting where there is also the assumption that he's only as attractive as his dick is big, that it's just something on the night's menu of choices. "There have been times where I've gotten down on myself when a guy comes over to me and my first thought is, 'Oh he must just have a preference for this.' Then there's the flip side, where I find myself attracted to someone and I want to articulate that there's more to me than the big uncut dick he finds so fascinating."

One night Danny told me about a guy he was impressed with at a party, a massively endowed white dude who chilled in a chair as a line of guys grouped around him for their turns. He was cool, this guy, calm and collected and able to sit back and allow himself to be desired. Danny had his turn, too, but he remembered thinking that though they all kneeled at the shrine and took their turns, interested as they were in the incredible size of the organ on display, not one person in the group referred to its color.

Size Matters

I'm sitting at lunch with two friends I'll call Anthony and Shelly.

Anthony is a gay guy who really believes that big is better. Anthony, who is white but dates *almost* exclusively black dudes, lives in Chelsea, goes out every weekend—if not every night—and has tons of sex. My friend Danny may have described himself as something of a size queen, but Anthony *defines* the phrase. Shelly is a cool biracial downtown gal, prone to funny asides and devastatingly observant witticisms. Shelly makes a point of dating guys of every possible race. They both like to talk about sex.

Around the time of this lunch, *Sex and the City* is about to go off the air and these two can't stop talking about the fact that one of the characters, Miranda Hobbes, had a long-term relationship with a black guy.

"White women rarely have love affairs with black dudes on TV or in the movies," says Shelly.

"Neither do black women," I say. "You know black men are incapable of love."

"Paul Winfield loved Cicely Tyson in *Sounder*," says Anthony.

"Billy Dee loved Diana in *Mahogany,*" says Shelly.

"And both of those movies are thirty years old," I say.

"I just love," says Shelly, "that Miranda told Blair Underwood that no one had ever been that deep inside her before."

"That show is *so* realistic," says Anthony. "Where else would you hear something like that on TV?"

Shelly says, "Realistic how?"

"About black men having big dicks," says Anthony. "You know, going deep."

"I don't know if that's true," says Shelly.

"You," says Anthony, "don't date enough black guys to know."

Anthony then tells us about meeting dudes online. "If a white guy tells you he has seven inches, he really has about six. If he tells you he has eight, he really has seven. But not the black guys. They tell it like it is. If a black guy tells you he has eight or nine? Believe me, sister, he has eight or nine."

"James Baldwin," I tell him, "says that the size is the color."

"James Baldwin," says Anthony, "must not have owned a ruler. I do."

I left lunch that day and, standing in the Starbucks on the corner of my street, I thought about my conversation with Anthony and Shelly and I sort of fell into Carrie Bradshaw mode.

Are black men's dicks really bigger than white men's dicks?

According to early versions of the famous Kinsey Reports, the average length of the erect adult penis is roughly 5.9 inches. Those early numbers were based on surveys that included primarily white men who held a postcard to their erect organ and dropped the results in the mail. Later incarnations of the Kinsey sex study, in which black men and other racial groups became part of the tested pool, indicated that the average length is closer to 6.1 or 6.2 inches. As reported by ABC News, according to information gathered by a mass study conducted by the folks at Lifestyles Condom Company—folks who, one hopes, consider penis length serious business—the number ranged from approximately 5.1 to 6.2 inches.

Checking around the Internet—where else would one go for dick talk these days?—I found a medical/information site called the-penis.com. Averaging the data from the studies and polls they'd collected, the-penis.com contends that black men tend to be about half an inch longer than white men, while Asian men measure approximately half an inch shorter than white men. There, in a list of myths that concern men about penis size, I discovered, after "Myth 2: Women Like a Bigger Penis" and "Myth 5: A Big Penis Helps You Make Love for Longer" was "Myth 9: Black Men Have Big Penises and Asians Have Small Penises," which supposedly isn't a total myth, they say at the site. Girth—the measurement around the middle of the penis—seems to "vary in proportion."

The information at the-penis.com is derived and adapted from "Race differences in sexual behavior: Testing an evolutionary hypothesis," a scholarly article from the *Journal of*

Research in Personality. The site continues with further findings:

> We averaged the data on erect penis size and found the
> averages to be approximately: Orientals, 4 to 5.5 inches
> in length and 1.25 inches in diameter; Caucasians, 5.5 to
> 6 inches in length and 1.5 inches in diameter; Blacks,
> 6.25 to 8 inches in length and 2 inches in diameter.

So the science tells us that black men measure—on average—perhaps an inch bigger than other men. Yet, like many things, when it comes to the public imagination, the myth carries so much more weight than the proof.

Most people will tell you: Yes, black men have bigger dicks than white men. They have bigger dicks than Asian men, Latin men, and any other race of men you can think of.

And it's not because they read the Kinsey Reports.

If I was a white person or Latin person or Asian person who didn't know any black people but saw such great movies as *Liberty Heights* or such silly movies as *Goosed,* where a naïve rich girl searches for a husband among a group of doctors, one of whom is African American, I'd probably assume that black guys are hung bigger than everyone else.

If one were to check out the Internet, one would definitely think that black men have bigger dicks. In several Google and Yahoo! searches, the words "big" and "huge" and "massive" almost always accompany any mention of "black dick." Though one will probably come across a few "big" or "huge" or "massive" Latin dicks, any other dick is usually either racially described with no mention of "big" or "huge" or "massive" anywhere nearby or simply mentioned as a "big dick."

Even the more sexually specific personals sites are affected this way, with many black men advertising their "huge *black* dicks" (italics mine) or potential partners advertising to find a "huge *black* dick" (italics, again, mine). In one hour of tooling around some of these sites, like the brilliant and popular Craigslist.org, I found, in one hundred and fifty straight scrolled-through postings, forty-five requests for or ads promoting "huge" or "big" or "massive" or, in two cases, "horse-hung" black dicks. I found exactly one reference to a "huge white cock" (from a guy searching for a black woman) and I found one mention of a "SuperHung White Stud" and his red-headed wife who were looking to invite a "hung" black or Latin guy into their bed. I didn't find one mention of—request for or ad selling—any "huge" or "massive" or even merely "big" Asian dicks. All other ads merely mentioned the guy being "well endowed" or "hung" or "average" or "not hung"—none of which had a racial adjective, even when it was clear that the person posting the ad was white or Asian or looking for a white or Asian guy.

It almost begins to seem like some cultural need, this emphasis on the hugeness of black male genitalia, as if the definition is there to settle the racial minds of both the definer and the defined. And it crosses the color line.

I used to joke that my life was like a moveable bar called the Color Line. I hang out at the Color Line every so often; I'm just one of those kinds of guys. Obviously, you meet a lot of white people at the Color Line. In fact, some of my closest friends are white, which might happen when you're a black dude who grew up on Long Island and tried to ply himself through the Ivy League and then decamped in Manhattan. Being at the Color Line isn't difficult. Sometimes it's downright fun, seeing how the other half thinks and talks and dreams.

You can learn a lot of things when you're a black dude chilling at the Color Line and you're willing to listen to what some of the white definers have to say.

I met this white guy who hangs out with a black buddy of mine, a white guy who thinks himself fairly "close to black"—because he played sports and knew how to breakdance when break dancing was all the rage—who is adamant that all black guys are hung bigger than every other race.

"I played football," he told me one night over Coronas at a little dive bar in the East Village.

I knew right away where this was going.

"So," he added, "I *know* that black guys are hung huge."

"You looked?" I asked him.

"You can't help but look when you got big swingin' dick like that right in front of you every day. Besides," he added, "all guys look. They're lying if they tell you they don't, you know what I'm saying?"

A few Coronas later, this guy, let's call him Ty, tells me that the main reason he knows that black dudes are huge down there is because *he's* huge down there. "And I check out other cats to see how I compare. Tell you what: I really compare to the black guys I've seen."

I ask Ty about being "close to black," if his huge dick has anything to do with this way he describes himself. And he laughs. Then he nods. And he tells me a story.

Ty met a girl named Helen. Helen was European. "French or Swiss, I don't remember which," he said. "I wanted to fuck this chick so bad I could taste it, you know what I'm saying? I was hot like that all night, from the moment I saw her walk into the club." After some flirtation, some dancing, and some drinks, Ty and Helen sat in a booth in the back of the club and kissed. Kissing led to groping. Groping led to unzipping. And Ty knew it was time to go. So he and Helen went back to his apartment. After some more unzipping, and undressing, down to underclothes for Ty and nothing for Helen, she grabbed him through his boxer briefs, smiled, and said, in her broken English—"which made it even sexier than you can imagine," said Ty—"Big dick. You hung like black man."

I'm hoping that it won't surprise you to hear that by the end of the evening, many Coronas later—and all protestations of mine aside—Ty showed me his penis. And, I can report, it was quite large. The look of pride on his face, the thrilled smile of success, of expectations met and surpassed, was definite. He didn't ask to see mine, much to my relief, but his smile told me that he didn't need to see mine; it was going to be as big as his, if not bigger, so crossing swords was not necessary. *The size is the color. The color is the size.*

Ty had measured up, had, in fact, spent his entire athletic life measuring himself against what he thought were the biggest and the best—even before stepping foot outside the locker room. He knew he'd been playing on the right field and didn't really need the competition to make any kind of play.

Would that all the white guys I've encountered in my life had been so endowed, for lack of a better word, with the ballsy bravado of Ty, who also told me, "Most white dudes think that not only black dudes are hung like horses, but that black guys are better lovers on the whole, and that hits cats where it hurts, you know what I mean?" As "close to black" as Ty thought himself to be—with his voice full of bass and his vocabulary street-toughed from years in the Race 101 lecture hall that a locker room can be—and as knowing as he seemed to be, there was also something controlling and naïve in his words. Ty was what I like to call an eracist—one of those racist people whose racism comes cloaked in the language of praise.

Ty listened to little hip-hop, read no black literature, socialized with few black people other than the friend we shared, and slept with no black women. Yet still he located his own sexual prowess—obviously an essential part of his makeup—in its similarities to black men. He might have been, as Baldwin wrote in his collection of essays *Nobody Knows My Name,* one of those white boys "trying to exorcise their terror of black men by, at once, instructing them and imitating them." Which is the very seed of eracism. American culture is laden with the image of what Norman Mailer named the White Negro, the cool-posing white dude affecting the presumed physical swagger and mumbled inarticulateness of black men. While the White Negro often arms himself with, at the least, a passing knowledge of black cultural tropes, or, at the most, a broad and redoubtable and all-encompassing in-sistence on honorary blackness, anointing a vaunted status to black folks that hopes to transcend racial differences, the eracist doesn't have an agenda of inclusiveness. His desire is to maintain status quo, to perpetuate the entrenched myths of blackness as a way of sustaining his own superiority, appro-priating the arguably positive aspects of those myths—strength, sex appeal—to bolster his own sense of self. The White Negro will seduce a black woman to reinforce his sta-tus; an eracist will market himself to white women as black-influenced. He's the mythically un-hung who uses the myth of the hung to make himself hung as well—thus erasing any status the mythically hung possesses. Ty referred to himself as "close to black"—but he'd never want to be black and has no use for blackness except as a sexual-cultural indicator that manages to dehumanize as much as he thinks it's celebrating. Even if Ty's words in our conversation were just his stab at a cool pose in the presence of a black guy who, in his mind, would probably only be his equal standing near the showers in the locker room, Ty might have, in one drunken moment, summed up the whole psychosexual history of the white male in relationship to his black brethren.

Those things happen at the Color Line. Sometimes I forget to carry my ruler with me. It comes in handy sometimes, which I first learned in college, after reading a certain body of text for the first time.

[In] childhood I envied Negroes for what seemed to me their superior masculinity, so I envy them today for what seems to me their superior physical grace and beauty. I have come to value physical grace very highly, and I am now capable of aching with all my being when I watch a Negro couple on the dance floor, or a Negro playing baseball or basketball. They are on the kinds of terms with their own bodies that I should like to be on with mine, and for that precious quality they seemed blessed to me.

—Norman Podhoretz ("My Negro Problem—And Ours," *Commentary,* February 1963)

As a black boy at a predominantly white university, I had already had enough experience around white folks to know that a lot of them had no shame when it came to the faint praise of black rhythm. You haven't lived until you've been a black guy dancing at a party with many white eyes on you, the looks of amazement enough to completely throw you off the beat. You don't want to let it get into your head like it does, but sometimes you can't avoid it. But avoiding it isn't ever really an issue. It isn't an issue because you don't have to be at the party: you can be sitting in the library, reading commentary on "race," and encounter elegantly articulated words like those above and know that some of the same people who think you "blessed" probably also believe that you're there at that university only because, for all your grace and rhythm, you fill some sort of quota. You'd once like to hear your people acknowledged for their "grace" under pressure or "envied" for their intellectual "grace," but ultimately you really don't care one way or the other. You just write—into the margins of the photocopied article—"or having sex?"

where the writer mentions Negroes dancing or playing sports with such "grace."

I wrote "or having sex?" in the margins of my reserved reading because I'd just had a conversation with some white guys about sex, which had resulted from a discussion we'd been having about rock music — about, more specifically, the Rolling Stones. We'd been debating the merits of the Stones versus the Beatles. Very typical undergrad conversation, as it was: Were the Stones really the World's Greatest Rock-and-Roll band or was that just self-applied hype on their part, a way to distinguish themselves from the studio-bound Beatles? It was a fun conversation, one of those late-night, coffee-soaked talks on the cheap carpet of the dormitory hallway. It was a fun conversation until I made a mistake. My mistake was race. And I don't mean my mistake was being black. Trying to bolster my latent music-critic argument in favor of the Stones, I'd jumped the gun and done something that white people did in conversations with me all the time: I introduced race into the discussion, citing the Stones' reliance on old blues to add color to their compositions, propping up my argument with my belief that the Rolling Stones had stolen everything they knew from old black blues records. With respect, of course.

My friend didn't trump me with the obvious, lobbing back the point that all rock and roll was stolen from old black blues records. He went right for the cross-court smash. "But the Stones are racists," my friend told me. "I'm almost surprised that you like them as much as you do."

I don't really recall how I defended the band after that

statement, but I do remember that we were joined by another guy as my friend proceeded to recite the lyrics to "Some Girls," the title song of a Stones album which had come under fire by black activists, Jesse Jackson most vocally. He recited the litany of lyrical descriptions that Mick Jagger had given to different types of "girls," stopping at the controversial, news-making couplet, to make his point: "Black Girls just wanna get fucked all night / I just don't have that much jam."

"That's racist," he told me.

"That's a point of view," I said. "Those are lyrics to a song, not entries from Mick Jagger's diary." Besides, I added, I heard somewhere that Jagger had said that the song was meant to be ironic, a commentary on how some guys might think about or describe women.

"They're still racist," I was told.

"But it's true." Those words came from the guy, the white guy, who'd joined our conversation as the lyric recital began. It was true, he told us, black girls *are* sexier than other girls *and,* from what he'd heard, they need it more than other girls. No offense meant, but from what he'd heard, that was the case, that was just how black girls were. "And Mick Jagger would know," he said. "He's been with black women." And he wasn't done: as far as he knew it was the same with black guys. Not only did black guys have big dicks but they also had more stamina than other guys.

"Now *that's* racist," I said.

Racist or not, it was true, I was told. And why would I get mad at that? That's a compliment, I was told. Black people have more rhythm and fucking is all about rhythm. Thus black people are better in bed. Everyone knew that.

"Have you ever been with a black woman?" I asked him.

He shook his head. "But I will one day," he said.

Suffice it to say, there wasn't much more conversation to be had, about race or the Stones or anything. Even after his apologies, even after he went red in the face trying to explain to me that he wasn't trying to be offensive, that he was trying to compliment me and compliment black women.

I was angry yet at the same time enlightened by the experience, by the actual casual presentation of stereotyping in my midst, by the sheer audacity of it all. The Racialization of Rhythm, as I'd called it in my journal, wasn't new to me, but the live-and-up-close articulation of it was. And thus, reading Norman Podhoretz on his "Negro Problem" (and Ours—uh, excuse me, Theirs), I was compelled to add, into the margins of my required reading "or having sex?" Because having sex was, at root, the behavior of the "Negro couple on the dance floor," was it not? Having sex, it appeared to me from knowing my American history, was the ultimate act of the black man, with his "superior masculinity," the sexual symbol, the plantation-bred breeder, the stud, the rapist. And always with such grace, "superior physical grace." At least, I'd told myself the first time I encountered Podhoretz's words, he'd been honest, admitting to his envy. But on rereading it, then and now, I'm always struck more by another word: watch. As in, look at. He'd gotten that part right.

Every black man knows about being watched. Considered. Observed. Profiled. Suspect. It's our birthright.

How's It Hanging in Hollywood?

"Thank God for HBO," says my friend Gail over the phone from Miami. "Where else would I get to sit home and see so many nude men I'm not going to fool around with?"

This does seem to be a period in history (pop-culture history, at least), when the unsheathed penis, full-frontal male nudity, seems to have come out of the censor's closet. It seems to have caught up with the bare breast as an expression of sexuality, of titillation. Richard Greenberg's *Take Me Out* had naked baseball players showering on the Broadway stage of the Walter Kerr Theatre. We've seen all the glory of Kevin Bacon and Harvey Keitel and Jude Law and Ewan McGregor in the movies and onstage. And on TV, between *Queer as Folk* and *Oz* (which stripped down everyone from rappers to TV stars to punk rockers as they all did tours of duty as prisoners), the male appendage has been front and center.

And of course there's the Internet. Nowadays you can go to one of thousands of sites to upload, download (or just shoot a load while looking at) pictures of your favorite male matinee idols in the buff, in stills (or "catches" in Net-speak), mainly from the movies in which they've appeared in the nude. There was a time when "celebrity skin" meant soft-focus female cleavage shots or perhaps a hint of scrotum between the hairy ass cheeks of some brave-hearted shot-from-the-rear pants-less guy. But not these days. Want to check out more than Brad Pitt's pits? Go to the Net, where paparazzi shots of a vacationing Pitt (in his Gwyneth-dating days) cavorting about are among the most downloaded images available. You want rocker Tommy Lee in all his well-hung Full Monty–ness? Go to the Net.

Where did this recent and fervent attention to the male package come from? Was this just the next step in pop culture's growth from weekend fun to global marketing phenomenon? Were we destined for this unsheathing, for these adventures in the skin trade? This isn't just a shift or updating, from *Porky's* (with its references to Pee Wee's "short-comings" and leering peeks through the shower-stall wall) in 1982 to *American Pie* (with it's pie-humping protagonist and semen-sipping antagonist) in 1999. It feels like a full-frontal assault on American culture. Is it because the men who govern everything are losing their grip on what passes for entertainment? Where once it was okay, at the behest of some ostensibly straight male studio heads and directors, for an actress to go topless, is it now okay, as women and gay men break the corporate glass ceiling, for men to bare all as well? Tat, perhaps, for a little tit? The dick has become its own man, so to speak, popping up here and there, battling the bare breast for supremacy, for sticky eyeballs, for asses in the seats.

One day I was watching the cable channel Showtime, and I was struck by two big-black-dick situations. On an episode of the now canceled *Soul Food,* a smart prime-time soap starring a glittering cast of beautiful black folks instead of the usual glittering cast of beautiful white folks, the show's narrator, fourteen-year-old Ahmad, found himself the object of sexual curiosity when two female classmates caught him on the soccer field in a moment of jockstrap adjustment and walked away giggling because they'd interpreted the bulge in his shorts to be a very big penis. Ahmad spent the rest of the episode dealing with questions of dick size and struggling with its relevance to his life. He was, it seemed, suddenly a teenager, vain and proud and insecure and amazed, staring at himself in the mirror, asking himself—cautiously? hopefully? willfully?—Do I have a big dick?

It's to young actor Aaron Meeks's credit that he managed to play Ahmad's curious and diverging emotions with such clarity and attention to pubescent detail. Ahmad's new girlfriend was changed by this information about him, suddenly, oddly, hesitant around him, at least until she worked up the bravery to ask him to show "it" to her, this marvel of maleness, this topic of conversation among the black teen set in and around the South Side of Chicago. Ahmad ultimately realized that his penis was normal, not too big and not too small, and, as with prime-time soaps, an hour later, there was some new drama to capture everyone's attention. The scene in which Ahmad shows his girl his penis, set in her backyard where Ahmad has been invited for lunch and a swim in the pool, had the classic and tentative coming-of-age rhythms familiar from hundreds of other TV shows, yet it had a certain electricity informed by the fact that the characters were black. Here was something new: a couple of middle-class black kids dealing directly with one of the age-old myths of black maleness in an awkward yet engaging way. Ahmad was somewhat familiar with the myth, and felt the burden of it, yet also found himself whipped into a little frisson of excitement at the possibility of what it all meant in the context of his burgeoning sexuality. It occurred to me as I watched that Theo Huxtable—the last TV rep for well-raised black boys—had never dealt with anything this Judy Blume–meets–James Baldwin.

(It also reminded me of the time I asked my mother why my dick got hard sometimes and was soft other times. Precocious kid that I was, there was no hesitation; I couldn't say the same for my mother. She sent me to ask my father, which I did. But before he could fully answer, my mother called him to the other room to watch *Columbo* or something.)

Ahmad on *Soul Food* doesn't know who to talk to about his problem, and then decides to try his hip uncle Damon, who stumbles around his mumbled words and never really comes up with an answer. The relief on Ahmad's face toward the end of the episode, when he realizes he's "normal" after all and not some freak of nature destined to be cruised by curious girls for the rest of his school career, is palpable; he relaxes into a cool-boy groove that makes him even more appealing to his girlfriend (who, it turns out, has her own issues about bust size, but that's someone else's book). That relief, Ahmad's passage to young black manhood, is made all the more real by the show's straightforward rendering of what happens when the mythically "hung" man has to realize that he might be merely "normal" and doesn't have to live up to some fantasy, for himself or anyone else.

No such reach for normalcy in *Good Fences,* a movie in which Danny Glover and Whoopi Goldberg play the Spaders, a black middle-class couple relocating their family to rich, tony Greenwich, Connecticut, in the seventies. They endure the perils and joys of upper-class integration, two children of the South now raising their children of the North with their eyes firmly on the prize of the American dream, though it often feels like some sort of satirical nightmare. The Spaders' son, Tommy-Two (instead of Tommy Jr.)—a good middle-class black kid being forced by his father to integrate himself into a lily-white ideal, yearning to graduate on to Morehouse instead of his father's choice, Princeton—is about to turn seventeen. He receives the birthday present of his life when the mother of his Japanese best friend seduces him during a sleepover. A sculptress, draped in a multicolored geisha-ready gown, Mrs. Suziharo asks Tommy-Two to be her model, then initiates him into the joys of sex. Standing before him, staring at him on his pedestal, her lips parted slightly, a look somehow both maternal and lustful in her eyes, she praises him on the size of his dick, exhaling wondrously at how large he is compared to "white men and Japanese men." What can Tommy-Two do but smile and accept his gift gracefully? Which he does—Coo, coo, ca-choo, Mrs. Robinson-san, Jesus loves you more than you will know.

It was a typical movie treatment of how a big dick is racialized. I watch a lot of TV and see a lot of movies, and I can only recall encountering one depiction of the big-dicked white guy in TV or movies: the hot-headed Sonny Corleone, Don Vito's oldest boy, in Francis Ford Coppola's *The Godfather.* It was part of Sonny's character, the bull in the china shop of Mafia negotiations, the philandering husband, bold enough to screw a woman at his sister's wedding—a woman, mind you, who we see early on watching Sonny's wife describe, with hand signals, the enormity of his member to a table of spellbound women. In the novel upon which the movie is based, author Mario Puzo describes Sonny as "so generously endowed by nature that his martyred wife feared the marriage bed as unbelievers once feared the rack." Sonny's cock was such a weapon, even a "hardened" and "fearless" prostitute requested "double price" after seeing it at full mast. Sure, the description is etched in the hot-blooded prose Puzo masterfully used to force his story into the world's imagination (and James Caan, in the movie, managed to personify Sonny's largesse without any skin even being shown) but it's also ace character development, foreshadowing the bullish behavior that will color the rest of the stories and influence the other characters.

But Tommy-Two? The fact that he is the least interesting character in *Good Fences* only highlights the sudden and abrupt attention to his penis. The fact of his largeness (in essence, his blackness) isn't played against the polite, subtly racist white people who decorate the New England town he calls home. And because we have no emotional investment in the horny-housewife character who indulges him with her compliments, the scene feels exploitative, blatant without being bold, coy without being provocative. It's an odd misstep in a thoroughly interesting depiction of black folks finding their footing on the ladder of upward mobility. Unless, of course, this abruptness was the point. Maybe Mrs. Suziharo was a Japanese Sula, letting Tommy-Two know that whatever else might greet him along the way, his dick was bigger than those of all the white boys in the 'hood. But I'd hate for that to be the case. Considering the large ideas that *Good Fences* is reaching for, Tommy-Two's sudden revelation as a hung stud dehumanizes him in a way that undercuts the larger implications of the film, trafficking in an almost blaxploitation-style abuse of otherwise powerful black tropes of identity.

Contrastingly, in *The Godfather,* Sonny's huge hangature is revealed early, so it becomes a point of reference for the way he bludgeons his way through the rest of the picture, informing his arrogance, his passion, his self-aggrandizing position of power later in the story. He's a walking phallic symbol compared with his more cerebral younger brother, Michael. Sonny's cock was a symbol of his own bragging, strutting cockiness (character development, if you will), the club he carried that made him more of a caveman when Michael's clever thoughtfulness is what will end up saving the family from destruction at the hands of their opponents in the Five Families.

Juxtapose Coppola and Puzo's wise and careful use of the Sonny character as a way of informing the story of family and pride and vengeance with the facile Tommy-Two moment in *Good Fences,* and the latter film falls disappointingly short in dealing with some of the same issues. It is especially disappointing because the movie has so much at stake, as both a historical document and a much-needed social commentary on race and class in America. In gritty flashbacks we see scenes of Tommy, Sr., as a boy being chased by redneck whites in the South, powerfully creating real and resolute reasons for why he has even brought his family to this place to suffer the slings that they do. The scene about Tommy-Two and his deflowering doesn't make us know him any more than we have up to then; it doesn't illustrate some point about his experience in the suburban 'hood he loves as a home yet loathes as a prison, the ostensible theme of the film as a whole. It sublimates rather than enriches the greater sum of his personality, and ultimately what could have been a powerful strand of the film itself.

I hate to be so hard on *Good Fences,* but as I get older the power of popular culture is becoming clearer and clearer to me, particularly the power it has to define how we learn about who we are. And I'm not talking about "positive images," that old sawhorse of passionate identity politics wherein the periodically downtrodden wish for only the most positive representations of themselves in the popular culture that defines and envelops the private and public imaginations. Who needs positive? All I ask for is smart. Too many of the negative images we see on film are neither positive nor negative, just dumb; they're unconsidered, received wisdom about people, places, and things we need to keep in circulation to maintain some relationship to the status quo. Usually all that's asked of characters in American films is that they "win," that they "succeed," which usually means "getting the bad guy" or "getting the girl." Both getting the bad guy and getting the girl are markers of American filmic masculinity in the Hollywood machine. Sometimes they happen together; sometimes they don't. That often depends on who's doing the "getting" and who's being "gotten."

In Hollywood, from what I've been told, there is this thing called "the list." The list is just that, a list. The list is something that stays close to the fingertips and hearts of the studio executives who oversee the writing, casting, and production of the product that reaches the screens and TVs of our lives. And because these executives control these things, they also control the images we get when we look at the screens. When it's time for a movie to get made, the list is referred to for possible casting suggestions. I have been told that Tom Cruise is at the top of the list, which means that any script that comes across the desk of any studio executive about to oversee a movie is immediately considered to be a possible project for Mr. Cruise. Being at the top of the list means that Tom Cruise can "open" a picture when it hits the screens, that he has a certain power to sway the audience toward inviting him into that public and private imagination that dictates which films will be hits and which ones will be misses. Being at the top of the list means that Tom Cruise has power. And he deserves it. Tom Cruise very often gets the bad guy and he very often gets the girl. And that's what we want when we go to the movies. We want a hero to be our proxy up there, battling evil, making good, tempting fate, running wild, winning ugly. But winning all the same.

Whether you're at the top of the list or not, in this culture we call ours now, the ultimate way to win is to be famous or infamous or just known, to grab a seat in the front row of public life. To reach cock-of-the-walk status, one of the swinging dicks of Page Six or *Us* magazine who's "making it." Culturally speaking, it's the ultimate paycheck, really, the gauge against which self-worth is measured.

It is telling, then, that the magazine *Details* chose to mention a "paycheck" in its May 2003 cover line about an infamous Hollywood piece of insider gossip that has taken on the level of myth.

Details—the celebrity-driven men's magazine that finds itself in a sort of ad-page game of big-dick "chicken" every month with a host of other glossy men's magazines like *GQ, Esquire,* and *Playboy,* as well as the British-imported "laddie" magazines like *Maxim, FHM,* and *Loaded*—seems to be the place to go for the slick-journalism version of what *Details* itself has called "dick-lit," a school of navel-gazing male-centric writing that usually spends its time glancing much lower, metaphorically speaking, than the navel. In a span of six months in 2002 and 2003, *Details* featured at least seven articles, many with eye-catching cover lines, about the male sex organ; it's become, with its glam fonts and screaming pull quotes, the place to go for dick info, for everything you wanted to know about dick but were afraid to ask lest your friends think you queer or your father smack you in the mouth. And based on the articles it seems apparent that men have reached the point where reading about dick goes deeper than the usual service-oriented pieces about the health of the male genitalia. *Details* has detailed proper urinal etiquette (when to look, when not to look, who to look at, who *not* to look at). *Details* has run the requisite "does size matter?" article (it does, according to many of the people interviewed). One article even offers ideas on how to make your dick look bigger (shave the pubic hair lower; use a vacuum pump; get surgery).

This cache of dick-lit, however, reached its zenith with the May 2003 issue, which also featured Scottish cover star Ewan McGregor. Right under the *Details* banner, in prominently bold black letters, reads the following: WHO'S THE BIGGEST STAR IN HOLLYWOOD? (IN THE PANTS, NOT THE PAYCHECK).

Hmmm.

The question one might ask is: Well, who cares? The savvy young male readership of *Details,* hip and happening and heterosexual twentysomethings who listen to lo-fi confessional music, shop at Fred Segal, and use expensive beauty products to accessorize their dirty Diesel jeans? (It should be pointed out, though, that *Details* doesn't seem to draw a line between its gay readers and its straight readers, often managing to cater to both sides in many of its dick stories so that no one feels left out.) The male readership of *Details* cares. Because magazines like *Details* are nothing if not bibles of aspirations, guides to the good life. And a list like this one—one of the oldest parlor games in the entertainment industry, old-school gossip that's been passed down from generation to generation of costume designers and loose-lipped ingenues (of both sexes)—is the kind of list that trumps anything *Forbes* could say about you money-wise. Financial fortunes can change. Hung-ness, the physical fact of it, lasts forever. And who doesn't aspire to that kind of notoriety?

"Who's the Biggest Star in Hollywood?" appears in the magazine as part of what the editors call a "Penis Package." The penis package also includes an article about Nude Male Casting, a California-based company that specializes in casting penises for full-frontal shots in movies and TV. Brian Carpenter's company places well-hung dudes into movies where the leading man isn't willing to show off his stuff or the director just needs some background dick to make a scene work. According to the article, Carpenter says he looks for guys with penises that bounce "off each leg as they walk through the locker room." Another article is about the "foreskin fanatics" at the forefront of the "foreskin reconstruction" movement. A sidebar article talks about how some men use human growth hormone to increase the size of their johnsons.

But the (family) jewel in the penis-package crown is entitled "Hung Hollywood" and features head shots of the most notoriously hung studs in the Tinseltown stable: *X Files* star and red-swimsuit-wearing David Duchovny (check out the episode "Duane Barry" to see what I'm talking about); the man in tights, Spider-man himself, Tobey Maguire (famous for an Internet-circulated photo of him with a penis *no one* would be able to hide in a pair of Spidey tights); Irish playboy-of-the-moment Colin Farrell; and Hollywood royal son Charlie Sheen, among others. All of these stars are reported to be on the hung list, a closely guarded list that has circulated around Hollywood since the forties, when Gary Cooper, John Wayne, Errol Flynn, and Milton Berle were all said to be hung—well, one supposes with the exemption of Berle—like the horses they rode in on. George Clooney is on the hung list, as are Liam Neeson ("look at the rope on that laddie," a crew member was said to have exclaimed when Neeson rose nude from a lake while filming a bathing scene in *Rob Roy)*, Bruce Willis, Jason Priestley, Matthew McConaughey, and others, some of whose heirs will probably still be hearing reported stories of their forebears' long manhoods well after their careers are over and they're dead and gone.

Hung, each and every one of them, the victim (or hero, one supposes) of many a dresser or sex partner's decision to tell all. Either that or the recipient of a bragging PR pro or generous friend who put the word out to keep his name in the papers and on the lips of the gossipy powers that be in La-La Land. Lucky guys, we might think. Not only have they broken the American-dream bank by parlaying their coy expressions and dimpled demeanors into fame and celebrity, they're also hung well, making it even easier to bed the people who need people to be famous in their lives. All these chiseled features, these secret agents and cowboys, cops and robbers, heroes and villains. We plunk down millions of dollars to see them in the movies or while away precious hours watching them on TV, and they're extremely well hung to boot. That is, if you believe the hung list.

But, on perusal, rereading the article, hearing the rumors, you get the feeling that something's missing from the hung list and all discussion of it.

Where's the brothas? Didn't any black men make the hung list? What? In Hollywood, a town that reverberates with the tremors of rumors that shake things up more than any earthquake, don't black actors sleep with or get dressed and styled by the same talkers who put this info out there? How is it that black men have the reputation of being the best-hung dudes on society's block but somehow went without mention in an article about famously hung men? Come on, out there doing the Hollywood shuffle, playing gangsters and criminals, hustlers and he-men, winning Oscars and Emmys and making us laugh with their quickness, black men are so invisible that they can't even get on a list of well-hung celebrities? Hollywood must be the only place in the whole wide expanse of this place called America—where, as James Baldwin wrote in *No Name in the Street,* "it is absolutely certain" that white men "invented the big black prick"—where a black man can't be as hung as his white counterparts.

Or can't, at best, be mentioned in the same breath. Because maybe this isn't just about Hollywood. *Details* certainly didn't publish the entire hung list. Perhaps this blackballing, as it were, is about something else. Did *Details* just not see fit to mention any black dudes? Did the editors of the "Penis Package" think the hung-est black dude they could mention would trump any interest in the beer-can thickness of that co-median who starred with Drew Barrymore in that comedy a few years ago? Did they think that it's somehow more un-usual, more newsworthy, perhaps, to cite only the white stars, to give props to that silver-tongued, silver-haired devil but not his angelic black co-star, who's reportedly *so* hung that two Bunnies ran screaming from a room at the Playboy mansion? That somehow people would find it more amazing, in a cul-ture where the stereotype sticks to black men like so much tar and feathers, to hear about hung white men for a change? Was this *Details'* way of recapturing the big dick, taking it back from black men, recasting it somehow as a feature of (white?) leading man–hood? Or was the article, the naming of those white-men names, an unwitting metaphor for something else, something more culturally sinister?

The hung list is really a list about leading-man success, about power, about the literal representation of an ephemeral quality that signifies authority. However evanescent the power might seem to be, though, culturally there is weight here: ac-tors, along with athletes and pop stars, are arguably the current standard for state-of-the-art humanhood, the new role models, the ones we look to, to tell us how to live, how to be, who to be, how to love, who to love.

Which means that the question of the hung list's missing black stars begs asking because all the men on the list do, for the most part, have something in common other than white skin. They're all, fundamentally, romantic leads, power players, leading men who squire leading ladies across the deserts and squad rooms and ballrooms of cinema screens around the globe. So the hung list points to another, bigger question, often asked yet interestingly reconsidered in this other context: Are there no black leading men in Hollywood? Thirty-five years or so after Sidney Poitier asked Hepburn and Tracy for Katharine Houghton's hand in marriage, are there any black actors who are card-carrying romantic leads, standing in for regular-Joe moviegoing guys in the public dreams that are movies, coming to dinner as the dashing fantasy date of the regular-Jill moviegoing women? Let's see: Will Smith is a box-office star, a leading man (though he still reportedly couldn't get cast in that John Grisham movie because, reportedly, Grisham didn't think he was "right" for the role). Wesley Snipes headlines at the multiplexes, though he's generally fighting and battling rather than loving and cuddling. Morgan Freeman gets lots of work, as does Samuel L. Jackson, and you can't read a celebrity profile of one of their white female co-stars without hearing at least one quote about how sexy and authoritative they are. You can add Morris Chestnut to that list or maybe Omar Epps or Mekhi Phifer or Taye Diggs, but whenever any of these guys "gets the girl," as it were, they do it in movies that are primarily niche pictures, marketed to exclusively black or urban audiences that cross over only rarely. They never intermingle sexually or romantically with women other than black women, and when they do, say Laurence Fishburne in *Othello* or Phifer in *O,* the prep-school-set updating of Shakespeare's less-is-Moor classic, well, you know the outcome.

Not that this is a plea for more interracial dating in American movies. Lord knows, just some good storytelling and fewer bombastic CGI effects would be progress. This is about sheer sex appeal, movie-star confidence, high-wattage bravado, or, simply put, star power. Long gone are the days when subplots involving blacks were cut out of films shown in the American South because white audiences didn't want to see black talent in films with white actors, yet somehow there still seems to be a version of this erasure at work. Particularly when it comes to sex and relationships. How is it that so many black men possess the majestic makeup of leading-man matter, the kind of powerful pull that draws women in, yet find themselves on the margins of the romantic scene, saving the world from alien destruction, vampire mafias, and, occasionally, white women from themselves, often getting the bad guy (or helping the white guy to get the bad guy) but rarely ever getting the girl in any major, blockbuster kind of way? It seems as if that would be the next step in so many of these stories. Watching Hollywood films with any sort of racial element, it's easy to feel that an entire component of leading-man life has been removed from them.

And one can only imagine that this is because these possible leading men are black men. One can only imagine that the powers that be, the executive-suite tastemakers, the people, as famously described by screenwriter William Goldman, who know "nothing," have decided that nothing further is required to make the black leading man, the probably hung black leading man *(the color is the size; the size is the color),* any more hung than he already is.

This is sort of like Ahmad, the teenager in that episode of *Soul Food.* This is what happens when the mythically hung isn't really hung—really powerful—at all. Perhaps there are no black actors on the hung list because there are probably few black actors on the other list, the one that resides near the elbows of those Hollywood execs. The eracist will cast the black man as the comic relief or the hard-nosed sidekick or the quirky sexual dynamo but rarely, if ever, as a true leading man. This black man can possess all the culturally sanctioned tropes of "blackness"—physical strength or grifter-savvy wiliness, the reformed con or the neutered partner. He can maintain a semblance of power but at the end of the day—and often of the film—he is ultimately disposable, dehumanized. It's almost as if audiences need some assurance that though the black man might be hung (sexually robust, virile) he won't ever be "hung" (powerful, desired, desirable).

Unless, his name is Denzel.

And he is desired, and desirable. You can't even begin to build a list of the black leading men without mentioning Denzel. Washington, of course, is his last name, like the Founding Father of our nation, but does one really need to use it? I can recall being at two events where Denzel Washington was present, a Sony Christmas party in 1995 and a birthday party for P. Diddy in 1997, both heavily attended by large groups of powerful white women—in Armani business suits

at the former, and Dolce and Gabbana catsuits at the latter—
and I remember hearing comments from women at both
events that showed me, before ever laying eyes on an episode
of *Sex and the City,* that women know what they want and tell
each other as readily as men do.

"If I wasn't here with my husband," said one woman at the
Sony party, "I'd be all over Denzel like white on rice. Damn,
that man is fine." It goes without saying that black women the
world over place Denzel on a pedestal of beauty and power so
high he'd be the first paraplegic sex symbol if he fell off. He's
already more talented than anyone on the hung list, a more
versatile, expressive, *complete* presence than most of the actors on Hollywood's A-list. But for the most part, Denzel's
career has been marked by a nobility that isn't much different
from the stoic diffidence shown by Sidney Poitier—at least
until Poitier's sly middle period highlighted by some smart
urban comedies—his closest comparison in the Hollywood
pantheon. And that's only because of the color of his skin.
Denzel is actually more in the Paul Newman vein, when you
look really closely at the work he's done. Stage-trained yet
loved by the camera, master of both the quiet burn and the
subtle rage, impossibly beautiful yet somehow accessible.

Check out *He Got Game* or *Devil in a Blue Dress* or
Philadelphia. Denzel's best moments, like Newman's, are
when the impossible beauty gets uglied up a bit, when he ex-
ploits the rougher edges of his game, exposes the flaws that
make noble heroes human. The best actor Oscar eluded
Newman until he revived, for *The Color of Money,* the slick,
streetwise Eddie Felson of his early career. The best actor
Oscar eluded Denzel until he unleashed the bad guy within

and scared Hollywood into realizing that the best actor in their midst was a black dude from the Bronx whose range (and rage?) exceeded their wildest expectations.

But before that anointed moment, Denzel Washington's career trajectory could have been defined by a moment in American racial times that felt like a step backward in history, even though it was touted as a step forward. In 1993, Denzel got the male lead in the movie version of *The Pelican Brief,* based on the John Grisham novel, apparently cast without regard to color, since the character of Gray Grantham was a white guy when the book spent months on best-seller lists around the world. What Denzel *didn't* "get" was "the girl," played by Julia Roberts, the biggest female star in the world, so big that she can pick which swinging dick will be her leading man when it comes time for her to make a movie.

There's an odd disconnect, though, as one watches the movie, particularly if one has already read the novel. One watches these two beautiful individuals, these movie stars, both hungrily "eating the lens," as they say, and never once are the sparks allowed to fly when you expect them to. Denzel, the intrepid reporter who can help Julia uncover the secrets that drive the film's plot, is Julia's helper, her protector, her port in the storm of her life, and that's all he remains. (It's been said that the studio bowed to pressure from Southern audiences who didn't want to see "America's sweetheart" locking lips or bumping nasties with a black man, a contemporary extension of how studios have kowtowed to Southern racists in the past.) Allowed to play the lead in the movie, opposite the biggest female movie star in the world who always "gets" her guy, Denzel is nonetheless kept from performing the final, and expected, heroic gesture, effectively erased from his own cinematic representation.

Never mind that the married woman at the Sony party would be all over Denzel like "white on rice." For all his success, it could be argued that Denzel will never be able to maintain a career in Hollywood in the traditional romantic-lead style because that would require a seismic shift in the cultural narrative, a need to make white men accept Denzel Washington as both a filmic representation of their own masculinity and as a repository for desire. White men would have to share the power, however ephemeral it might be. But is that asking too much? If audiences were allowed to ride the waves of their cinema fantasies with Denzel Washington manning the ship, that seismic shift in the cultural narrative would open the floodgates, inundating the shores with a boatload of black heroes to save the day. As fundamentally liberal as Hollywood represents itself to be, the conservative method it has of ensuring that black men never get to be on the hung list of leading men—in this case, the A-list of heroic and romantic leads—is imbedded very deeply into what James Baldwin called in *Playboy* in 1985, "the American ideal of sexuality [which] appears to be rooted in the American ideal of masculinity." According to Baldwin,

This ideal has created cowboys and Indians, good guys and bad guys, punks and studs, tough guys and softies, butch and faggot, black and white. It is an ideal so paralytically infantile that it is virtually forbidden—as an unpatriotic act—that the American boy evolve into the complexity of manhood.

In other words, we're right back there in *Liberty Heights,* with the preteens warning their white buddy away from the black girl. Because he can't compete with the swinging dick of the black dude in the locker room.

Denzel and Wesley and Morgan and Will and Samuel L. have made and will continue to make millions and win awards and grace the placards outside mall multiplexes. They may have wives in their movies, waiting patiently at home for them to put out fires and kick some ass, but they will never swashbuckle the Hollywood heroine who plays on their level. They will never share in the true spoils of romantic heroism.

Or maybe they will.

Just this year has seen Will Smith, arguably the current biggest star in Hollywood, have another major hit with *Hitch,* a romantic comedy that cast him as a relationship expert teaching men how to get their grooves on. Smith has carried a good-guy label his whole career, even as a rapper, emphasizing the "wholesomeness" and "unthreatening" qualities that make him ripe for across-the-board Hollywood appeal. Since hip-hop has lately been the site of so much black male sexual braggadocio—as well as the newly mainstream music of choice for audiences of all colors and classes—perhaps Will will be the future of the black man as Hollywood lover? Perhaps he will lead the pack of rappers-cum-actors like Ice Cube and Treach and L.L. Cool J who have also found themselves as romantic leads opposite sexy, charismatic females. Either that or Denzel will have to keep working with black directors like Spike Lee *(Mo' Better Blues, He Got Game),* Antoine Fuqua *(Training Day),* and Carl Franklin *(Out of Time)* to find the sexy stud within.

Then again, cut to the Academy Awards, 2001. It's a night to remember: Sidney Poitier is the honored elder, perched in a balcony seat, the king of all he surveys. Halle Berry wins best actress. And Denzel Washington wins best actor. As a pop-culture moment, it's the triple crown of black popular-culture dominance, sort of like that night at the Grammys in 1983 when Michael Jackson walked away with everything— pop, rock, rhythm and blues—for a record called *Thriller*.

Who announces Denzel's name at the podium, on this, the biggest stage that the movie industry knows? Julia Roberts, America's sweetheart herself, fairly shivering with the opportunity to bestow upon Denzel Washington the highest honor in the land. It's positively orgasmic, this display of love, of friendship, of honor. You can't help but hear all those times Julia's stressed how much Denzel was the best co-star she'd ever had, how she couldn't believe *she* had a leading actor Oscar and Denzel, up to that point, didn't.

It was a wonderful moment to behold, watching power eat the lens with such ferocity. It was a wonderful moment to behold because history was being made at that moment. Not the history of a black man winning the best actor Oscar—no, that had been done before. What America saw that night, on the biggest stage Hollywood knows, what was confirmed for America from the lips of it's very own sweetheart, was what they do know in the executive suites where they don't know much else, and also what Denzel and Will and Morgan and Wesley and Samuel L. already know, and that was this: whatever else ever happens with the roles of black men in the Hollywood-sanctioned space of the public imagination, hung list or no, Southern audiences or no, there is one tenet that everybody knows:

Once you go black, you never go back. Or better yet, when are Halle and Denzel going to star in a movie together. Now *that* would be hot.

Putting a black man on the hung list fulfills a stereotype. Not putting one there confirms a lack of power. But, at the end of the day, the *Details* article about the hung list is just that, an article, right? Just a little dick-chat in a world full of dick-love and dick-envy, in the pages of a magazine that probably meant the whole piece as a diverting piece of fluff that shouldn't be taken too seriously. Maybe. But if a black dude can't even get a shout out about the most dangerous, tantalizing, curious, damning, convenient, and, frankly, according to many brothers, appealing of stereotypes thrown their way, what gives? If a black man can't even measure up in the let's-talk-about-dick scene that passes for American culture at the turn of the new century, if the lust and interest that gets masked as fear and loathing remains the status quo, what exactly can a brotha do?

Maybe the blaxploitation period in Hollywood got it right.

If anatomy is, in fact, destiny, if what's hanging between your legs is a disrespected, degraded symbol of your hyper-stereotyped manhood, envied and abhorred and desired, a worshipped totem of your feared power, don't keep them wishing, hoping, thinking, or wondering what's down there.

Get busy already.

Shaft, Mandingo, and Other Assorted Superstars

We are products of our time. And the products of our time are instrumental in inventing who we are. The products of *our* time, three totems of self-reflexive community building and self-reflective identity building, have been sports, movies, and music, popular sites of public imagination that have grown and survived as much as marketing behemoths as they have artistic ones. It could be argued, thanks to the recent globalization of these products, that almost everything the world knows about black men it has learned by watching black men in these most presentational of modes: dribbling, defending, or spiking a ball; strutting, shooting, or grinning across cinema screens; crooning, toasting, or rhyming into microphones.

My dad was a kid when Jackie Robinson broke major league baseball's color barrier and became a hero to a generation of black folks who were lucky enough to be born at a time to witness one of these cultural firsts. Yet, privy as they were to firsthand stories of those strong-willed superheroes who contributed to the continuing invention of the black man, they were also treated to a portrayal of black men in movies as weak or ineffective or just plain invisible.

I was a kid when many of the stars of blaxploitation flicks were athletic dudes, transplanted from the heroic fields of dreams that is American sports. Jim Brown, Jim Kelly, and Fred Williamson, among others, had found original success as athletes, and brought their hypermasculine energy to the celluloid world, trading in their jockstraps and sneakers for firearms and fly fashion, and, filmically at least, building even higher cultural monuments to the idea of the black masculine ideal. They had to. Saving the inner city from the scourge of drugs or protecting black people from the evil white empire, these superheroes weren't only rescuing their people from the man but also reclaiming an entire filmic history from the castrating cultural czars who'd defined the black man in movies up to that point. Sure, we'd had the success of Sidney Poitier, and even Harry Belafonte and Brock Peters, among others, but the heroic black man, putting out fires with gasoline as it were, fighting hard and loving harder, was an almost new concept.

Even though I was considered something of a sissy in my youth, more interested in reading a book than tossing or kicking a ball, my earliest memories of movies—and, ultimately, my earliest memories of black heroism—are completely intertwined with sports. My Saturday afternoons at the local movie house—remember those?—were spent watching football stars–turned–movie stars Jim Brown and Fred Williamson create bigger-than-life personalities that defined the cinematic representation of black masculinity. The dialogue they spoke was beside the point—and barely heard anyway underneath the constant commentary that permeated the usual talk-back-

to-the-screen moviegoing style of the black folks I was sur-
rounded by in the theater.

Instead it was all about the body, the way in which these
strapping bucks fought and fucked and careened around
the scenery like they were still on the gridiron. This was the
beauty of these films, it seemed, and their appeal: it was a
spectacle of black male movement, the unspoken ways in
which black men took up space in a world that seemed eager
to erase them from it by any means necessary. There was a
disconnect for me personally, yet as much as I cherished the
word, spoken or written, as much as I craved narrative sturdi-
ness (even at that young age—yeah, I know, sue me), I was
nonetheless carried away by the appearance of these brawny
brown-skinned brothers and the strength of purpose that over-
rode the literary conceits I'd come to associate with movie
storytelling. I was enthralled by the sheer force of will they
exuded and, indeed, was eager to take my karate-kicking part
as Jim Kelly when my buddies and I reenacted scenes from
Three the Hard Way in my backyard as lightning bugs lit up
the night.

To be heroic was to be athletic; to be athletic, of course,
was to be a man. *The Greatest* (featuring Muhammad Ali);
*Cornbread, Earl and Me; Fast Break; The Fish That Saved
Pittsburgh*: many of the movies were sports-themed, whether
comic or tragic, and so often likened black male salvation to
the ability to play sports. Here was the black man as con-
queror, as able-bodied stud, an updating of previously prescribed notions of black masculinity, yet refashioned and
recast to portray the ability as some sort of populist pro-black

spectacle that nonetheless still reinforced white viewers' stereotypical ideas of black "power." The defining trait of athleticism could manifest itself, not only in playing sports but also in the ability to fight and fuck, to unleash one's masculinity in a rhythmic and crowd-pleasing way that only *seemed*—with the movies' wayward "black power" politics and "hip" street language and commitment to "edge"—to make new the very old and dated ideas of "strength." Black men were "strong," physically imposing, big. All perfectly fine adjectives to describe a man. But the cartoonish ways in which many of these qualities were presented were, ultimately, not the most progressive means by which to instill real pride into the building of a real black nation. White folks watched these films and decided that the inner-city black male spoke pimp English fluently and thought of "whitey" as a weaker, less virile version of himself. Black folks watched these films and—is this any surprise?—mostly thought the same things. The explosion of blaxploitation films had brought the slick quality of black-brother cool to the hinterlands, sent the shrapnel of new stereotypes flying out of reefer-scented jazz clubs and glitter-balled discos into the wider world. The fetishizing of cool as a race concept had been ratcheted up a notch.

Perhaps it started with *Shaft*.

The idea that Richard Roundtree could portray a cool black detective named Shaft before the mid-seventies explosion of urban black cinema is, in retrospect, positively mind-blowing. His triple-entendre name—referring, one supposes, to his dick, his gun, and his tendency to use both of them to get his way—linked to his street-legal intellectual prowess managed to straddle the fine line of racial exotica and hero worship and ensured that, with that mix, it could only be a hit movie. A black man who loved as hard as he worked, who was "for the people" and yet "a man alone," who crushed a cherished filmic stereotype of black male ineffectiveness yet cruised along on an assumed stereotype of black male hypermasculinity, Shaft convinced the drug dealer to work with him to save the community from a larger, more lethal white-run power structure. He had Black Power politics, he had virility, he had athletic grace, he had a big dick. Shaft was not *a* man, he wasn't even, to be real, *the* man. No, taking no shorts, convincingly incorruptible, Shaft was the New Black Man, kicking off the seventies stylishly, the Black Dick cool enough to have Isaac Hayes provide his personal sound track.

Even though he could fight and fuck with the best of them, "cool" didn't quite describe the other totemic black male figure of seventies cinema, the one whose name would be borrowed by porn actors, who's muted dynamism might have been of his time, who (as it were) spoke little and carried a big stick, whose name became synonymous with the myth of black men, used by blacks and whites alike to describe black penile virility. His name was Mandingo and he arrived on movie screens across the nation in the very middle of the decade.

Here's the thing about *Mandingo*: Mandingo, as the stud slave portrayed by boxer Ken Norton (another athlete-turned-thespian) came to be called, the iconic representation of black male hung-ness, was actually named Mede, as in short for Ganymede, described in Homer's *Iliad* as the "handsomest of mortals, whom the Gods caught up to pour out drink for Zeus and live amid immortals for his beauty's sake." There are different versions of the Ganymede myth, depending on which version of the story you encounter (the Archaic Greek version or the Hellenistic myth narrative), but the basic story remains the same. Ganymede was simply, purely beautiful, the most beautiful creature that Zeus, king of the gods, had ever seen. And Zeus, married, as it were, to Hera, wanted Ganymede for his very own.

Living among the mortals of Troy, Ganymede found himself kidnapped by a soaring eagle — Zeus in disguise. The eagle swept Ganymede off to Olympus to live among the Immortals, first as Zeus's lover, much to Hera's jealousy, and then ultimately as the cup-bearer for all the gods. Eventually, as reward for his sexual service to Zeus, Ganymede was made an Immortal himself, becoming the constellation Aquarius, the water-bearer. All the better, it turned out, as Hera had finally gotten fed up with this beauty taking her place in the king's bed, and declared war upon Ganymede's fellow Trojans as revenge.

Crammed full of betrayals and love affairs, family strife and grand gestures, the Ganymede myth, like other myths, has its roots in real emotion, in lesson-teaching parables that sometimes read like guides to living. Replace Ganymede with a nubile young female and you can almost picture him being portrayed by Debra Paget in some big-budget Cecil B. DeMille costume epic, casting serene glances at, say, Anne Baxter (in full *Ten Commandments* Nefertiti mode), as she slyly takes her place in the castle. This story of lust and revenge among the privileged set could take place even in some heavy-breathing Douglas Sirk epic, in glorious Technicolor, starring, say, Jeanne Crain and Lana Turner as, respectively, wife and mistress, battling for the heart of some gray-flannel-suited cad of a man.

Yes, let's go with Sirk here, because *Mandingo,* released in theaters two years before the TV version of Alex Haley's *Roots,* and close to forty years after *Gone With the Wind,* remains, in my mind at least, the definitive cinema take on master and slave, and it's done with the kind of overripe melodrama you might find in a Douglas Sirk film, only without the attention to surface slickness that those soap operas formally demanded for the world in which the story took place. *Mandingo* instead plays out its sordid story mired in the muck and mud of a decaying Southern plantation circa the mid-1840s, and the decadent filth of the set design gives the story an even more squalid and debauched quality in which the Ganymede myth undergoes a narrative inversion. Here, the Mandinka slave, eventually to be named Mede, would not fall into the bed of his master, the young Hammond Maxwell, who is actually all the while falling in love with Ellen, one of his slave "wenches." Mede would become the bed toy of Hammond's randy wife, Blanche, who is bored by plantation life after a rousing life in the city of New Orleans and jealous of Hammond's relationship with Mede as Hammond trains Mede to be a fighter on the bare-knuckle slave-fighting circuit.

Mandingo is a hard film to watch, mired as it is in filth and misery, reveling as it does in its taboo subject matter, full of full-frontal male nudity and cross-racial sex and its endless use of the word "nigger," which the actors spit out with a peculiar blend of high-minded disregard and almost operatic flair. Watching it again recently after having first seen it in the late seventies on TV, it's interesting to think that Muhammad Ali was first approached to play Mede. Ali definitely had the beauty needed to make the Ganymede analogy work, but his keen ironic sense, not to mention his well-expounded political opinions, would have sucked the soap-operatic life out of the piece. It's also hard to picture Ali sitting still for the overly fetishistic way that the movie portrays Mede's body, the glistening, greased-up, muscular frame that is nothing more than a money-making, climax-inducing object of both ridicule and desire, chopping down forty-foot trees, winning fights, thrusting between the legs of his plantation mistress.

When first we meet Mede, he's on a slave block, chained and waiting as the plantation owners peruse him and others for signs of weakness, for any sign that their eventual purchase may not be worth the price. At one point, young Hammond and some other male owners watch as a burly German woman inspects Mede (called up to now the Mandinka)—and inspect him she does, reaching underneath his loin cloth to grab at his testes, a look of orgasmic interest in her eyes. You get the feeling that the Mandinka will be doing double duty on *that* plantation. And so do the men watching. Hammond, in the market for a fighter, outbids her. It is understood that Hammond buys the Mandinka for his reported Mandinkan strength, but it is also understood that there is no way Hammond or any of the other male buyers there will let this woman use this slave for her own sexual pleasure.

That this woman should be using her money to buy her own pleasure knows no place in this patriarchal system.

Particularly since this here Mandinka, soon to be called Mede, is "hung so big he'd tear up the wenches." And of course it's understood that Hammond creeps down to the slave quarters to dip his stick into some slave girl's "honeypot." That the movie attempts to engage on this level of gender difference, of the psychosexual dynamics that lead a plantation owner away from his white wife and into the slave quarters for sexual fulfillment because the white wife is a "lady" and the slave is a "wench," gives *Mandingo* a weird kind of seriousness that you want to resist; that it eventually engages these issues around motivations of love and not just lust gives it an even weirder kind of depth.

What's interesting about *Mandingo,* though, is the way it straddles so many different American movie styles and still manages to maintain such a singular and streamlined mess of a vision. In its slavish devotion to clandestine sexual entanglements, it plays the heaving-bosom tropes of a historical romance novel, mixed with a bit of old-Hollywood plantation-era historicity; it's *Gone With the Wind* if the Southern gentry drank Colt 45 instead of mint juleps. By laying race upon this structure, through the relationships between the masters and the slaves, it attempts to lay claim to the blaxploitation seventies, hanging a scrim of (then) new-Hollywood Black Power onto a stage already littered with the remains of some of the ugliest race-baiting imagery ever seen on film: this is a film, wouldn't you know, that has an escaped (then eventually captured) slave yell to his lynchers, "After you hang me, kiss my ass!" yet opens with shots of the plantation's master, played with decadent regal splendor by British actor James Mason, sitting on the veranda, his bare feet planted firmly on the belly of a little black boy lying prone before him like a hassock, because this was the best way, we learn, to get the rheumatism out of his feet. By building up the relationship between Hammond and Mede, the crippled white-boy slave owner and the strapping fighter-slave who stands by his side, *Mandingo* even has "buddy flick" elements, though those elements are a cruel setup for the ultimate act of sexual "betrayal" that eventually leads to Mede's end. *Mandingo,* sort of like Hammond, wants it both ways—fearing the virility and toughness of the big black man, yet respecting it enough to bond. *Mandingo,* like Hammond, wants to love the slave and whip him, too.

Above all those movie conceits, however, *Mandingo* just might be the ultimate American sports-race picture, the perfect metaphor for the black male athlete and his conflicted, complex relationship to mainstream American culture. If in fact the black man *does* get reinvented every so often in some new cultural form, *Mandingo* wants to invent the notion of the athletic black guy and the way in which his athleticism removes him, perhaps dangerously, from the other hordes of black folks around him. Before there was the first black heavyweight champ Jack Johnson and his white wife, before there was Muhammad Ali and his clever race-man articulateness, there was Mede, Mandingo himself, bare-knuckling his way across the American South, a bull of a man, a beautiful savage, named for nothing less Olympian than a Greek mortal who eventually became a god. From its Greek mythology references to its anachronistic modern context for black guy/white guy sports-buddy clichés, *Mandingo* is about, at its heart, the black athlete as god.

That's the Way the Balls Bounce

Extraordinary black athleticism being magnified through the
lens of media is nothing new, harkening back to the days of
Jack Johnson's dethroning and thorough thrashing of white
champions in the ring. To bring it closer to home, Jackie
Robinson defined my dad's generation, while my generation
will be defined by Kobe Bryant and Mike Tyson, Wilt
Chamberlain's declaration of his twenty thousand lovers, and
Sports Illustrated cover stories detailing the boom in "illegitimate" kids by numerous athletes (some white but mostly
black). We had the showtime Lakers of the eighties, but we
also had Magic Johnson and his announcement in November
1991. We had Dennis Rodman. The concept of "date rape"—
a term I first heard at college, and thus came to associate with
drunken shenanigans on messy frat-house beds—took on national prominence with the faces of black athletes attached
as poster boys of bad male behavior. The concept of "baby
daddies"—a phrase I'd heard around the way, referring to the
fathers of kids born out of wedlock, usually used in the plu-
ral—took on national prominence, tarnishing the reputations
mostly of black athletes who couldn't, at least in the media's
eyes, keep their dicks in their pants in the mid-nineties. The

concept of AIDS and HIV—up to then associated almost solely with the presumed promiscuity of white gay men and the injudicious behavior of drug users—suddenly had a new face, the eternally smiling, defiantly heterosexual face of Earvin "Magic" Johnson. The concept of pure-D freak became defined, in a pop-culture context at least, by rebounder extraordinaire Dennis Rodman. In the nineties, there sure were some wobbly pedestals on the Mount Olympus that was black sports superstardom. Even Michael Jordan, the god of gods, found himself the source of whispers about his own extramarital sex life. Suddenly it seemed that the often unspoken link between sports and sex moved from cultural subtext to CNN news fodder. We already knew that black men were bred to be good athletes—Al Campanis had educated us in that respect and lost his job in the process. But now we had the invented role of black men as sex champs linked to the also invented role of sports champ, and the bull—no pun intended—ran wild in the proverbial china shop.

Sure there was some difference in the way Tyson and Bryant were regarded in their new media-appointed roles as "rapists." Tyson's reputation prior to meeting Desiree Washington in that Indianapolis hotel room had already been defined in terms of brutality and violence—he is, after all, like *Mandingo*'s Mede, a boxer, prone to seething outbursts, street fights, brawls. Kobe, on the other hand, was a smooth, lithe, Italian-speaking suburban boy, so Michael Jordan–manqué that he might as well have stepped out of a video game; he was a hero of mythic media proportions. Yet each man, now aligned with a brutal sexual act—like Michael Jackson during his 1993 battle against child molestation charges—found that the discussion of his penis had become part of national discourse. Defenders of Kobe Bryant called into nationally syndicated radio chat shows to say that all that happened was that Kobe's dick was "too big" for that "little white girl" he was "trying to do." I remember reading articles about the Tyson trial which mentioned the "largesse" of Tyson's "sexual organ" and how he'd "forced entry" onto Ms. Washington. In my lifetime, I have followed media coverage of sensationally played rape cases—William Kennedy Smith, Alex Kelly, and Robert Chambers, among others—and never once do I recall any mention of the penis of any of those guys, and most definitely not the size of the penis of any of those guys. Apparently, in the Kobe and Tyson cases, it seems as if we hadn't come far from the phallic fantasia that was *Mandingo,* and the scene at the auction block. Had the size (and, of course, the color) of the penises involved in these cases somehow been the cause of the case itself? The sex life of the American athlete: add "black" as a modifier and suddenly we're talking about promiscuity and disease and violence. Somewhere between Kobe and Mike Tyson, football star Mark Chmura was accused of raping his children's teenaged babysitter. Never once do I recall the size of his dick coming into the national conversation. But, of course, it wouldn't. There is no national fascination with the dick size of Mark Chmura. Partly because, unlike Mike Tyson and Kobe Bryant, there is no one, in the national imagination, being protected from the dick size of Mark Chmura; there is no body of literature, factual and fictional, detailing the possibility of sexual violence lurking inside Mark Chmura, linked to his race, linked to the invented notion of what damage is possibly done by the mere presence of the thing dangling between his legs. Kobe and Mike Tyson's crimes break an unspoken agreement between mutual benefactors: the black athlete and the white mainstream (usually male) culture that embraces them. When race becomes part of the debate, it almost always seems like *Mandingo* all over again: the black athlete will submit to ascribed rules that are set up: you be black and do what black guys do (be virile, be strong, be worshipped), while I'll be white and do what white guys do (be worshipful, be deferential, yet always be more powerful).

It's a pact made in the shadow of the tall trees that line the strange and twisted American cultural landscape, rife with the hanging ghosts of black men who stepped out of line, who where forced to relinquish any agency, any power, to a more powerful presence. So often, when this pact gets broken, when the black athlete steps out of character or out of line, we hear the "lynching" card being played, the idea that a black man, dissed in the crucible of American psychosexual politics, has lost his power, has experienced what Clarence Thomas called a "high-tech lynching." And in all the talk one hears about penis size in the context of these deal-breaking alleged violations, one thinks of James Baldwin's words from *No Name in the Street*: "What did you want to do with my dick when you cut it off after lynching me? Did you want to dye it darker and somehow attach it to yourself?" Or perhaps we think of Eldridge Cleaver again:

The Omnipotent Administrator conceded to the Supermasculine Menial all of the attributes of masculinity associated with the Body: strength, brute power, muscle . . . Except one. There was this single attribute of masculinity which he was unwilling to relinquish, even though this particular attribute is the essence and seat of masculinity: sex. The penis. The black man's penis was the monkey wrench in the white man's perfect machine. The penis, virility, is of the Body. It is not of the Brain . . . By and By the Omnipotent Administrator discovered that in the fury of his scheming he had blundered and clipped himself of his penis (notice the puny image the white man has of his own penis. He calls it a "prick," a "peter," a "pecker"). So he reneged on the bargain. He called the Supermasculine Menial back and said, . . . "Look Boy . . . I must cuckold you and fetter your bull balls . . .

I asked a friend of mine, a former NFL player, about my "pact" theory, about the power dynamic between the watched, worshipped black athlete and the watchful, worshipping white hordes that fill stadiums across the country. He told me this: "When you play ball on that level, from college to the big leagues, even starting in high school, you're black, but you're not really black anymore. You sort of transcend race."

I think of Mede, the stud in *Mandingo,* who suffers hot brine baths "to toughen up his skin" and lives in the slave shacks, yet travels long distances from the plantation with his master to make money as a fighter, who is considered to be "something special," yet is still a slave.

My NFL friend continues. "The thing is, that ability to transcend race, so to speak, makes you think you can get away with anything. You're pretty much taught, and you begin to believe, that you can exploit that difference. You can exploit the fact that because of your skill on the court or the field or whatever, that you're getting treated like other black men aren't getting treated. You feel privileged."

Privileged. Is that how Mede began to feel? Particularly when he was called into the main plantation house to become the boy toy of Miss Blanche, the mistress of the house, filling her with the dick she's not getting from her husband, Hammond? Of course, Blanche is pulling Mede into her own soap opera here. Of course, Blanche is jealous that Hammond's real love is the beautiful wench in the slave quarters. And she's jealous that Mede gets to travel on the road with Hammond, at his side, sharing, for all intents and purposes, his interests and life. Of course, after weeks of sex, when Blanche, as is her prerogative, cries "rape," what exactly is Mede feeling? We never really know. Mede has made the pact, but he's never given any agency in the narrative.

And Mede gives "potboiler" a new definition when he's beaten and thrown into a vat of boiling water as punishment for his crime, for breaking the pact, for being bold enough, slave enough, to be with a white woman. There is never triumph in Hammond's face as Mede meets his end. There is a look of confusion and guilt, as if for him Mede was suddenly made human, that for all his beauty and strength and virility, he was, like Hammond, just a man, a myth made small in the dirty reality of their lives. Just as Hammond didn't know himself, at the end of the day he didn't know Mede, outside of the slave-warrior he'd invented for his own means.

As part of our conversation, I tell my NFL buddy my reading of *Mandingo*. He's not impressed. He thinks it's just a slave flick from the blaxploitation days of the seventies. What he does tell me, however, is this: "It's not just about white folks."

"Which means?" I ask him.

"Which means," he tells me, "that we trade in the same stereotypes all the time, we as black men. And that's why we get into so much trouble sometimes. What you said about a pact might be true, but it takes two sides to make a pact. And all that talk about Kobe, and all that talk about Michael Jordan back in the day, the only way that can happen is if both sides agree. Let's face it, white folks get mad when something goes wrong in these athlete situations because they think they know. Everybody, especially the media, they think they know Kobe or Michael. But they really don't. They know what the commercials say and they know what the image is. But they don't really know the person."

Before I can respond to what he's said, something else pops into my mind. It pops into his head, too.

We say it together: "O.J. Simpson." And we burst out laughing.

It's fairly understood these days that the O.J. Simpson imbroglio of the mid-nineties was as much about a big black man and the sex he had with a blond white woman as it was about, well, murder. O.J.'s alleged acts, brutal and bloody and full of rage, shocked the nation and his eventual acquittal drenched us in the flood of angry opinions about the use of the race card and its attendant abuse. What always floored me about the O.J. Simpson story, however, was the way in which so many white folks who were shocked—shocked!—by the "playing of the race card" were unable, as it were, to believe that race *would* play some part in the outcome of the trial, which was perhaps one of the most racialized, widely viewed trials in the history of American culture. It was almost as if the fact of O.J.'s "blackness" was a card trick, a surprise, some kind of bizarre third-act plot twist in the Court TV–ized drama that the trial became in the nation's consciousness. O.J. *had,* in the marketing, gridironed glory sense of the word, transcended blackness, had reached that pinnacle of African American success where putting asses in stadium seats and making people laugh on multiplex screens had anointed him with a sort of cultural pass to the high life.

But the moment he was arrested for a crime of passion, the mantle of "blackness" shrouded him like a dashiki. *Time* magazine blacked him up for its cover shot. Callers at radio and TV chat shows decried his violence toward the "beautiful" Nicole, some even asking whether this brutal behavior of O.J.'s wasn't some kind of reaction to his own conflicted relationship to his experience of privilege. Apparently, for white folks, the playing of the race card was then some kind of betrayal, a world-changing fall from innocence. It wasn't fair for him to be "black" now after all the years of being allowed to be neutral when it came to racial identification. It wasn't fair to slay the prize of white womanhood after he'd been rewarded with that prize for so many years of service. I remember a friend of mine telling me that of course O.J. Simpson killed Nicole Simpson. My friend thought that O.J. had been driven insane by his own Mandingo fantasy, that, in his mind, the mere possibility that Nicole had decided to spread her legs for someone like Ronald Goldman, someone who couldn't possibly measure up to the big-dick pleasures O.J. had been good for, drove the Hall of Famer insane with jealousy.

It was a result of my friend's O.J. theorizing that I really began to think that the black man was some kind of cultural invention. I'd always suspected it—that to be a black man was to live in a world that was like a carnival house of mirrors, with every version of the black male experience reflected and refracted back at the black man, with him forced to choose which experience to use to his best advantage to get out alive. For those of us modern enough to be inundated with the constant orgiastic imagery of movies and TV and music videos and magazines and twenty-four-hour news, we had a long list of cultural signifiers from which to invent ourselves. If *Mandingo* was the best my friend could reference as a description of O.J. Simpson's state of mind, if, in fact, *Mandingo* could still be the cultural reference for the sexual dynamism of the big black buck with his big black dick, we as black men had surely lost the latest round of signifying. Because in *Mandingo* it's Mede, the Mandingo figure—not the white plantation mistress—who is the de facto "raped" character, the violated character, yet it is Mede who's still thought of as the aggressor. Somehow that's been lost in *Mandingo*'s move from cultural artifact to cultural touchstone. Either that or we as black men have given it away.

We as black men love the strength of *Shaft,* and how it defined us in the public imagination. But we also love the length of Mede, which, up until *Mandingo*'s release and because of its taboo nature, had been more a matter of public stereotype given power by private fantasy. Historically there has been a certain strain of sexual eroticism around black female sexuality in American culture that gets played out in some public arenas—I think of, say, Josephine Baker's randy stage antics, or "artistic" representations like the Venus Hottentot, or even the disco-era vinyl orgasms of Donna Summer's "Love to Love You, Baby"–"Bad Girls" period. This exoticism historically *could* be played out in public arenas because the public imagination—its gaze—was so defiantly and powerfully male. There is and was public space, however complicated it could get considering the complicated role race plays, for the desire and manipulation of the black female image, because as an invention of desire rather than an invention of power politics the black female sexual image was less obviously threatening to the general power structure.

The hypermasculinity of the black male sexual image was ironically an invention designed to emasculate. By creating a sexual monster, they'd created something that needed to be controlled, feared. If that was the case during slavery and Jim Crow, sadly defined by lynching as a way to control the invention, the post-mid-century explosion in American culture of racial and gender grasps for power—civil rights movement, women's lib—resulted in a realigning of the politics of desire. Suddenly control—the public imagination and any discourse about it—wasn't just in the hands of white men. There was a public space for a new sexual exoticism of black men, mainly found in the communally consumer-driven worlds of sports and movies and music. In other words, though *Shaft* may have been made primarily for inner-city black audiences and though it provided a sort of power platform from which black men could reinvent their image, there would be in *Shaft*'s wake—*Black Caesar, Hell Up in Harlem,* and others— the model for a future of cultural production that understood only too well that the invention of the black man could be as complicated and fraught with tension and dissonance when it was black men themselves doing the inventing.

White men may have invented the black man in America, but brothers eventually got themselves into the lab, too, and the lessons learned weren't always good ones.

Don't Peek/Just Looking

I was at a dinner party in early 1998 in Los Angeles, and the conversation, as it's wont to do when you're at a dinner party in Los Angeles, turned to movies. A bunch of us, mostly the New Yorkers in town to work or beg for work, went outside to light up post-dinner smokes. Someone asked me what I thought the ten best movies had been in the last year. Pop-cult obsessive–slash–movie freak that I am, I started to reel off my list: I loved *Titanic* more than anything, and I loved *Chasing Amy* and *L.A. Confidential, The Full Monty* and *Eve's Bayou* and *Deconstructing Harry.* Oh yeah, and *My Best Friend's Wedding,* and *Donnie Brasco.* I tossed *Good Will Hunting* in there, too, if I remember correctly. What I recall best is that at first I couldn't come up with ten. Someone at the party, another smoker, a white dude I'll call Hal, said, laughingly, "Those are almost all white movies."

You could have heard an ash drop.

Someone, a white person, said, "And your point is?"

"My point is," said Hal, "that other than *Eve's Bayou,* I thought he'd name more black films."

"Because I'm black?" I asked him.

"Well," said Hal, all eyes on him, "yes. Because you're black."

There was some obvious discomfort for a little while, not from me. These things, like I said earlier, do happen at the Color Line. I was actually used to this kind of thinking, from white folks and black, who never knew what to make of my tendency not to cast my every endeavor, interest, or argument in a sheath of African Americanisms. By this point in my life, I'd ceased to be amazed by some white dude's surprise that my tastes somehow didn't fit into his notion of what they should be.

This was pointed out when someone said, "You don't know Scott. His tastes run the gamut." I didn't need this person's defense of my "tastes," but I let it pass. What I didn't realize, however, was that my "tastes" had actually unspooled (and would continue to unspool) a new thread of conversation—the race conversation—when I said, "I also really liked *Boogie Nights*." That was my tenth pick. "Another white film," I added, before my new friend Hal could say anything else.

"But there were black people in it," he said. I sensed he was just trying to be difficult. "The Don Cheadle character and the black woman who was a porn actress."

"Her name was Nicole Ari Parker," I said to Hal, and then I added, and I don't know why, "You know what was strange in *Boogie Nights*? That we never saw Don Cheadle's dick."

"Because the movie wasn't *about* him," said Hal. "It was about Dirk Diggler."

"But he was a porn actor in it, too."

Someone then said, "There was a black guy in *The Full Monty*."

"And he had a really big dick," I said. "He was called Horse."

"Actually," someone else said, "I think it was the repairman guy who had the big dick. He had no rhythm but he was really well hung."

Apparently the *Full Monty* comments, which were meant to sway the conversation away from the tension between Hal and me, hadn't done their job, because Hal asked me, "Was it important to see Don Cheadle's dick?"

The tension was back.

It wasn't to me *personally,* I explained. "I wasn't making some sort of challenge to your, or Dirk Diggler's, white manhood," I told Hal. "I wasn't trying to make it a competition." I just found it interesting, I explained, that a movie about the porn business would cast a black actor and *not* emphasize his dick as part of the plot. I found that sort of refreshing.

"I found it refreshing," Hal finally said, "that the white guy did have a huge dick. You always hear that about black dudes but you never hear it about white guys."

I thought I'd come to a nice little dinner party where I'd meet some people and make some new friends. Who knew that dick size and race would be the topics du jour? I really didn't know how to respond to Hal's words. So I said, "Well, in a post-Mapplethorpe world, I guess we need more *Boogie Nights* to, you know, even the playing field."

I got some laughs out of that, and I figured I'd made my point. I was about to head back into the restaurant when Hal said, "What's Mapplethorpe?"

———

Boogie Nights may not have been "about" Don Cheadle, but Robert Mapplethorpe's *Black Book* would have provided him with a starring role.

Then again, I don't know—I'm not sure exactly how hung Cheadle is.

I first searched out *Black Book* because, completist that I am, I'd heard that the foreword was written by poet/playwright Ntozake Shange, famously the author of *for colored girls who have considered suicide when the rainbow is enuf*, and that the foreword would include a new poem by the lady herself. This was, I can say, at the height of my "black women writers" phase of readership, when everything I put my hands on to read, other than, say, the novels of Stephen King, was by some passionately direct and terrifically meaningful black woman writer. I'd plowed through all of Toni Morrison and Alice Walker and Paule Marshall. Shange's jagged edge of a voice, beautiful in its blend of anger and defiance and love, purely and simply redefined what poetry was for me. The other reason I'd searched out *Black Book* was the other, first *Black Book,* the book-length history lesson of black folks' lives, crammed full of photos and letters and drawings, that Random House had published in 1974. I'd flip through the book at my friend's house, breathless at the breadth and scope of it; it was an encyclopedia of love in my eyes.

I can't say I knew a lot about this Mapplethorpe guy at that time. I seemed to recall seeing the word "controversial" next to his name in *The New York Times* or *The Village Voice* when I was a teenager, but I had no referent for his style or the content of his work. But if he was working with Ntozake Shange, he had to be at least sort of cool in his worldview. (That was a word I'd learned recently, too, "worldview," as in an artist's worldview and how politics and culture might influence an artist's worldview.)

Well, I found the book. And what I found was a collection of nudes, a portfolio of photographs of naked black men. I can still remember standing in the bookstore in Manhattan, my mouth agape at the impossibly graphic images. They'd started off innocently enough, shots of a shaved head, a muscled ass, a greased-up torso cropped right at the beginning of the groin, a pair of balletically arched feet, a sweaty profile. Then the shot on page eight, the skinny guy with the Afro, his heels pulled up to rest on the edge of an industrial-looking chair, his knees akimbo to reveal his uncircumcised penis. This was the first penis but it wasn't the last. Of the ninety-seven photos in the book, twenty-six of them featured some kind of crotch shot. There were all kinds of penises on display: big ones and bigger ones, dark ones and light brown ones, cut ones and uncut ones.

The most striking image in the book, for me, was on page fifty-five, where I found a shot of a brother in a three-piece polyester suit with his big veiny uncircumcised dick hanging out of the open zipper. No head, no feet, the shot was cropped at the chest and the thighs, the big dick the very center of the frame. What struck me most about the picture was the element of cheapness it had, the way the suit gripped the model's body, as if the suit was so confining that his dick had to swing freely. Was this a comment on inverted middle-class servitude? Had the photographer put the model in this suit to reveal something about the black man's rejection of straight bourgeois signs? Was this a fuck you to the powers that be who would force the black man into playing a role that wasn't, really, in his cultural repertoire? How did I know? What, in fact, did I really know about art criticism?

Not much. But what I did know about, innately maybe, was subjectivity. I must have, because it dawned on me, standing there in that bookstore, that these photos hadn't actually been taken by a black man. There was something about the pictures, something distancing *and* distanced, that struck me as posing, as if the photographer was posing as much as the models were. There was something in the posture of the models themselves that struck me as positioned, in a way that didn't seem completely natural and at ease, as if they'd been caught in the act of being black. Maybe it was the greased-up body parts. Maybe it was the hood over the head of one of them. Maybe it was the way some of them seemed to be showing off. I turned to the back of the book, and sure enough, Robert Mapplethorpe—the man with whom Shange looked, as she'd written in her foreword, "for former lovers" they both "knew were somewhere in the book"—was a white dude. I stared at his photograph for a while, trying to figure out how he managed to seem so flintily hard, in his pompadour and tuxedo jacket, yet sort of pristine and angelic around the eyes. He looked to me like a soldier—there was something formal about him, his head turned just so, his eyes fixed on the camera (and me)—but a soldier who'd been to the front, who'd seen some battle, who had stories to tell. I turned back to the photos of the black men in his book to see what those stories might be. And that narrative had exactly one thread: these brothers have put all their business in the street—and did it for a white guy. I hope he paid them really well. And I remember thinking that only a white dude could get away with publishing a book full of big-dicked black dudes and get Ntozake Shange to write a poem for it.

I closed the book, put it back on the shelf, and got on the train at Penn Station and returned to campus.

It was a year or so later, on campus at Brown, that I encountered Mapplethorpe's *Black Book* again. A friend had a copy of the book and it became a sort of totem, passed around with fervor. I can remember that the last time I saw that particular copy it was tattered almost beyond recognition. Pages had been razored out of it and taped to dorm-room walls, others shared with embarrassed giggles, others jerked off to I imagine. I describe the book as a sort of totem because it had come to represent an emblem of those of us, the tribe of us, who had originated its existence among our peers. We were an "edgy" crowd of artists, sexually subversive and adolescently self-conscious. We had a reputation for outspokenness, a notoriety for self-expression that we encouraged with fervor. Once we got past the conversations about the dick sizes of the models, there were the conversations about "beauty," about the sheer physical presence of so many of the models in the book. But there were other questions: What about the guy in the leopard-skin throw and the hunting stick? What did he mean? Was this some statement about black male savagery, some jungle-bunny joke being played on *Black Book* readers? And why so many pedestals? Was Mapplethorpe some kind of fetishist? Were these black men being celebrated? Or were they being denigrated, posed to expose what America had been taught to believe about black men, that we were all hung and studly, built like running backs with big thighs and muscular legs and pecs that could barely be contained in regular clothing? The questions were mixed with the continued giggles. There were those of us who took the *Black Book* for what it was (or was supposed to be?): ninety-seven photographs of black men in various stages of dress, as a coffee-table accessory that might complement some nice phallic candles. We thought these were just terrifically composed photos of terrifically endowed brothers who were as beautiful as the male species got. Then there were those of us who were stuck on the fetishism thing, referencing Shange herself from the foreword: "Black men, black-and-white prints of said black men, overshadow other obsessions." As far as we were concerned, the black male body had already done its time as an accessory, as an obsession. Why should it be stuck in the pages of this book like the iconic representation of some white dude's obsessive fascination?

I was somewhere between the two camps. Like Shange and Mapplethorpe, I wanted to believe, as she wrote in the foreword, that I "understood passion and good form are a constant gratification." There were photos in the book that held the terrible beauty of a black man's "good form," where the lissome lines of leg muscles were like spectacles of black maleness captured. I could only imagine prints of the photos hanging in some gallery, their glossy and hung images for sale under the hot bright lights of buyers' eyes. I was there in the middle, trying to reconcile my burgeoning education in loving art with my duty to ask questions that would give the art some meaning. And I did have one question that nagged at me just about every time I looked at *Black Book,* those times when I really felt as if I was "looking" at *Black Book,* rather than appreciating it. What was up with that hooded figure?

That was my question because around the time of the appearance of *Black Book* in our lives, around the time I was studying art and its relationship to cultural politics, I was also studying history. And around the same time I saw that photograph of that lynching, of those white folks laughing and looking up at the hanged black man.

Looking.

Oftentimes the victim was the hooded figure in the tableau.

Here in *Black Book* was a hooded black man at essentially the very center of the book, on page fifty-four, in a photograph called, simply, "Untitled 1980." Here was a black man, his thick dick hooded in its uncircumcised state, his hands meeting at his chest, his head sheathed in a hood of indeterminate material. He can't see you looking at him. But you're not looking at him, you can't see his eyes, you're looking at his dick. You can't desire him, because he's been reduced to a featureless phallus. Or is that why he is desirable? Would anyone find this desirable?

Here was the notion of "hung" writ large: a well-hung black man wearing a hood—akin to those worn by both the racist terrorists who lynched black men and the black men who were lynched—in a photograph that could ostensibly be hanging on a wall in a gallery. It wasn't hard for my mind to make the jump to photographs of lynched black male bodies, knowing that underneath the baggy pants, where that dark spot is, there may not be a penis. It might have been taken, a

The man in the hood (Untitled, 1980) from Mapplethorpe's *Black Book*

representation of his emasculation, a comment on how his hypermaleness had been chopped down to nothingness, as a means of social control, as part of a spectacle. From the inspection of his genitals in slavery, to the thievery of his genitals during Jim Crow, to the framing of his genitals in *Black Book*: each and every action existing on a stage, tied to its audience in a theater of cages, fear and loathing transformed into an erotic moment of celebration.

I wasn't in the middle anymore. And I couldn't look.

Pass the Remote

Looking.

I'm a man and like most men, I operate visually. I like to look. I get off on looking. But I'm also a black man, which means I'm looked at as much as I look. It's the Invisible Man myth, which was probably why looking at Mapplethorpe posed such a conundrum for me. Here were these black men on display, caught in the four thin edges of the photographs' frames like exotic creatures robbed of their scientific and cultural specificity. And rather than just appreciate them as art, I felt culturally violated. Was this similar to the feminist reaction to pornography, that strange bastard child of filmed erotic art with its own set of detractors and supporters on any and every side of the political spectrum? Was this like the feminist position that no porn was "good" or "necessary," that all of it was "exploitative" of women? Perhaps, perhaps not. This was high art, after all, not pornography. This was posed photography, shot for critique and appreciation (and probably some shock value), meant to be shown in spaces stamped with the imprimatur of culture. This wasn't just naked people meant to titillate. That's what *porn* was for. Which posed another conundrum for me: I thought of myself as a feminist.

And I thought porn was cool. I thought it could be problematic. I thought it could be mean and shallow and ripe with ridiculous ideas about sex. But, like most men, it was where I learned a lot—at least I thought so. I also thought it was fun.

Until I discovered a film that forced me to think a little differently, forced me to look at porn as a vividly evocative site of analysis, particularly if your life is the Color Line and you're interested in the politics of the intersection of race and sex.

It really should come as no surprise that one of the biggest black stars in porn—an industry that uses the phrase "hung like a horse" like a mantra—is a man named Jake Steed.

And Jake Steed's work might be the most evocative of them all. Among other work, Steed is the producer and director and star of the popular and celebrated series *Little White Chicks and Big Black Monster Dicks*. Compactly muscular, corn-husk brown, with a perpetually jaded sneer of a smile and the sardonically arched-up eyebrows of his handsome face, Jake Steed usually stars as the ringleader of a roving band of brothers made up of some of the biggest studs black porn has to offer. The *Little White Chicks* series follows Jake and his crew as they search out lonely/bored/horny white girls and sexually ravage them into submission. These are gang bangs, often shot in a raw handheld style, almost like home movies, sometimes taking the POV of any of the Big Black Monster Dicks and rarely taking the perspective of the Little White Chicks, who, it seems more often than not, are whisked away to some alien location to partake in their desired gang-banging.

The movies have the washed-out graininess of hostage footage and the leering, sometimes masked faces of the gang-bangers move teasingly, winkingly, in and out of the frame, almost daring the viewer to comment. On the sound track, the black actors' voices are slowed down and deepened, so that they sound like beasts from some other world, not just black guys tapping some white ass but instead growling, laughing monsters. There's an idea that film semioticians have about audience identification, or "subjectivity," that comes to mind watching the *Little White Chicks* movies. Using concepts of Lacanian psychoanalysis that theorize on the role of the spectator as an active participant in the film-watching experience, movie analysts find certain cultural and political implications at work. They call it social "positionality." If I had to name a social positionality at work for the viewer of the *Little White Chicks* movies, I'd call it "man who'd been cruelly sent the footage of his ravaged wife or girlfriend in the mail." If the assumption is made that porn is created for men, created for the man to lust after the woman, to thus identify himself with the masculine presence there in the scene with the woman, and if we believe—as I've been told by experts—that the porn-purchasing public for movies like this one is 70 percent white men and 30 percent "other," then are we to assume that there is a sizable audience of white men lusting after a product that portrays white women being sexually ravaged by a tag team of extra-hung black men?

It is, it seems, an odd inversion of the Hollywood method.

The assumption in Hollywood is that white men don't want to watch, say, Denzel Washington *kissing* Julia Roberts. Yet here is an explicit representation of that dire cultural stereotype— the marauding sexual black beast—selling some of the largest amounts of product in the marketplace.

Says porn producer Bill Marigold *(Hot Chocolate),* who helped shepherd in the rise of interracial porn videos in the early to mid-eighties, much of the black and interracial porn is produced chiefly for the white porn consumer. "That more blacks are viewing this material is purely accidental," he says. "When I put blacks in my videos, I project my fantasies, not theirs."

Is this Norman Podhoretz watching with envy as the rhythmic Negro couple dances? Or at least the Negro man? Is this the guy from my college conversation identifying the prowess of the hung black man? Is this the primal representation of the white male inferiority complex writ large across the screen?

Watching these men, many of them members, it seems, of what's called in the porn biz the Beyond Ten Club (black porn actors hung close to, at, or over ten inches), do damage to these white women, I experience as odd a disconnect as I get watching Denzel Washington *not* seducing Julia Roberts in *The Pelican Brief,* but in reverse. I want to find some political statement in them—particularly since Jake Steed reportedly propagates a very pro-black cultural and political stance in his private life—but an active search for that political statement feels forced and wrong. This is about desire—not the desire for black men to participate in the degradation of white women but the desire of white men wanting to watch (and symbolically participate in) the degradation of white women, using a big black stud as the weapon of choice. And yet beyond just finding the scenes erotic or pleasurable as porn, they do have a dramatically political effectiveness I didn't expect. If white men had, as Baldwin wrote, invented the idea of the "big black prick" for his own control of the black body, to demonize the black man as he simultaneously fetishized his "difference," it made a weird and perfect sense that a white man would be turned on by the site of his "invention" doing his dirty work for him.

"The guy who's watching these films is thinking 'If only *I* had a big dick like that, that's what I'd be doing to her,' " I was told by major porn star Lexington Steele, a sometime actor in the *Little White Chicks* series. He adds, "We get glorified for that." Glorified, essentially, for creating a canvas on which a white man can make a display of both his desired sex object *and* the object of his envy.

I ultimately have to disregard my own disconnect from the film. I'm not the audience for it. The audience for this film series wants the stereotype to be in play, needs it, in fact, to get off. It's a virtual power play of complicity: he can have his dominance *and* his envy; he can play out his own inferiority yet feel superior as well. This isn't a condemnation. This is about desire.

And isn't that one of the tricky things about desire? As much as desire can't—actually, really, shouldn't—be policed, it can still find itself handcuffed, shackled to history and skin color and myth and all the attendant specificity and volatility inherent in the bars that build the cells we try to keep it locked away in. But even if this is the world of porn, with its own twisted logic about sex and desire, it isn't immune to the same sort of hyper-racial sensitivities you might find in Hollywood, particularly as it's a place where race and sex and money intersect.

As popular as the *Little White Chicks* series is, as popular as some of the brothas who perform in those films are, there are still white actresses who will not perform with black male porn stars, sometimes because of their own cultural prejudices, but often at the behest of their managers. Lexington Steele has a name for this dichotomy, for the contradictory way that porn has of using myth to sell a fantasy, yet will also use that myth to bring everything crashing down to reality. He calls it "phallic jealousy."

Phallic jealousy is part of the sharp legacy of sexual jousting that has impaled the very heart of American culture, as informed by the politics of gender as it is by deeply rooted historical factors of race fear. In a weird way, the resistance that white "name" actresses have to working with Lex or other black actors actually spouts from the very same fount which demands that he *does* fuck white girls, all bound up with the ancient push-pull of miscegenational sex. White men buy films of white actresses getting screwed by big black men, yet there are white male managers in the porn business who don't want their white female talent to work with black actors because they feel that such exposure will hurt these women's chances of being a major star in the game.

Which, it seems to me, makes for as interesting an example of economic control as it does racial control. These films sell extraordinarily well, yet the white actress is kept from performing in them because her presence in them might negatively affect her career. What she loses in financial rewards, she gains in racial currency. On the flip side, it hints that the black male actor can effectively portray a rapist but he cannot portray a lover. What he gains in financial rewards, he loses in racial currency.

If you ask black male porn actors about this, you find out that there are more than just economic concerns at work here, and perhaps this is their way of taking back some control in the equation: "major" white female porn stars are kept away from black male porn stars because their managers—very often their husbands or boyfriends or some sort of significant others—don't want them to get turned out. According to Lexington Steele, "In this industry, white guys just don't want their white girls feeling the big dick that they don't have. That's phallic jealousy." He added, "It's basically an inferiority complex. Any white woman who's fucked a black dude has always come back for more or has spent a lot of time trying to come back for more. *White men know that.* And they feel that the 'black animal' won't have 'this one,' meaning one of the pure white girls who has managed to become a star."

So this is about, as it historically has been, protecting the virtue of white womanhood—the sacred object of white male desire, of *everyone's* desire—from the dangers of the big black beast. But that isn't the entire story, is it? The fear isn't just in the hearts and minds of the white women—who, it appears, often don't have an agency of their own when making these decisions. It's in the white men. If you look sideways at the notion of penis envy—Freud's explanation of a girl's reaction to her own femaleness, how she's envious, wanting to replace a "lack" with a real and desired "presence"—it looks a lot like phallic jealousy. And white men, history has shown us, anointed black men with the hypermasculine role that is, cleverly, as corrosive as it is celebratory.

How awful it must be to have invented the big black dick, then to have to spend so much time ensuring that it doesn't overshadow one's own sense of self-worth, that it doesn't somehow destroy your own stature. What's a white guy to do, when his leading-man position is on the verge of possibly being usurped?

Well, you can always create a new myth to conquer an old one.

You can always create a hung list.

In an industry that prizes the very thing that, symbolically, keeps a Denzel Washington off the hung list—the looming possibility that he hangs better and is just waiting to unleash that hangature on the world—Lexington Steele is a bona fide leading man. In an industry in which women are the main attraction, in which female faces (and other body parts) are the selling points that move product, Steele is a star. With his massive fan following and record-setting three best male performer awards from the *Adult Video News* (a sort of porn version of *Variety*–meets–the Academy of Motion Picture Arts and Sciences), compared to other men in the porn biz who are mainly, mostly, studs for hire, Steele reigns supreme. He is a tall, pitch-perfect evocation of what singer India.Arie affectionately calls "Brown Skin." He is also a perfect evocation of that love-cum-envy that Toni Morrison's Sula detailed so incisively—because, to put it bluntly, Steele is not only model handsome and athletically built, he is also hung, very well hung. Lexington Steele is eleven inches hung. Eleven-by-seven inches hung.

On the list of brothers in porn's unofficial Beyond Ten Club, Lexington is said to come second, after Jack Napier, and before Sean Michaels, Jake Steed, Byron Long, and Justin Slayer. He may come second on that list, but if you ask around, many porn aficionados will rank Steele higher, partly

Lexington Steele, a part of porn's unofficial Beyond Ten Club

because of his superior bedside manner and partly because, when compared to other guys in the porn business, he is the whole package. Steele can pull it off, no pun intended. "It" being the ability to perform, which in the world of porn is more than whipping out the dick and stuffing it wherever the director instructs it to be stuffed. "It" is that highly regarded ability to be hard on cue (reportedly less stressful lately with the advent of Viagra), to be ready to shoot—in both senses of the word—when the director is ready to film, to be able to act the scene and make it real for the audience.

As provocative as a big dick might seem to us laypeople, size isn't always what gets a guy into the porn game. "Size almost pales next to performance," Steele told me one August night. "Next to the ability to shoot on cue or last longer to make a scene work? A big dick might get you in the door, but that ability to really perform is what keeps you in the game."

That ability to perform well has made Lexington Steele more than one of the most popular porn actors to grace the cover of a DVD case. Steele is one of the few porn actors to successfully make the transition to director/producer/owner. With Mercenary Pictures, the production company he founded in 2002, Steele has some control over his image and how his films get produced and distributed. Though he's had success performing as the Impaler in a series of films, appearing in the *Up Your Ass* series and guest starring in Jake Steed's mega-successful *Little White Chicks and Big Black Monster Dicks* franchise, Steele has given the world under the Mercenary banner *Lex Steele XXX, Black Reign, Top Guns, Super Whores,* and *Lex on Blondes*. His triple-threat status as performer/producer/director doesn't just make him a brand name to be reckoned with; it also provides him with a clever and clear-eyed way of looking at the business of porn. When he told me, "This is a business and as a performer you look to penetrate a market," it is clear that he appreciates the intended pun and appreciates that I appreciate it. "You also look to maximize your potential as a brand. You know that you're filling a void and that you're giving the audience a fantasy, but that doesn't mean that I'm not aware of what it means that I do what I do."

That awareness might come from the unusual way he made his way to porn. Before Lexington Steele was Lexington Steele, a king of West Coast porn production, he was a suburban East Coast kid, from Morristown, New Jersey, a middle-class, churchgoing kid who didn't have girlfriends but excelled at sports (and lettered in three) before graduating from high school and first matriculating at Morehouse College only to eventually transfer to Syracuse. No girl-friends? "This was the late eighties, early nineties," he told me. "It was still all about the light-skinned, curly-haired brothers. The world wasn't safe for the shaved-head dark brother yet."

After college, where he pledged the black fraternity Omega Psi Phi, the stereotypically rowdier-than-thou Q-Dogs, Steele took his degree and landed on Wall Street, trading stocks and bonds for Oppenheimer. He did some modeling, the "legit" kind with his clothes on, but that didn't last. He was, simply, too big for the sample-sized clothes models were expected to sell to buyers and shoppers on the runways and in the photo shoots. Not too big *down there,* but in his broad shoulders and long legs. Someone suggested that he try modeling for some adult publications and those jobs led to the suggestion that he try his hand at the porn biz. Which certainly was a place he'd never hear that he was "too big" for anything. So, in 1998, with enough money saved to last him, he figured, three or four months, he headed west, and there he remains.

His first few jobs, as it is for black dudes arriving on the scene, were primarily in all-black productions, doing sex scenes with black women. But he wanted to move into the interracial market, mainly because it paid more money and could only broaden his audience. And, like he'd told me, he was aware of what he was doing and, most important, aware of what was needed of him. "White consumers have certain expectations," he told me. "The idea of the big black buck deflowering the little virginal white girl is very popular." Steele could do the "deflowering" but he also learned that as much as the audience may enjoy that scene, there was an irony at work that didn't completely surprise him. To "deflower the little virginal white girls," producers hired a specific sort of black man. This was the *other* part of the package: along with the big dick and the ability to "perform," Steele, like other black guys who wanted to work the lucrative interracial market, had to be what he calls "palatable." "Nonthreatening," he told me.

Interesting concept: black men hired to be the big black buck had to be nonthreatening and palatable enough to appeal to the white men who wanted to jerk off to images of little virginal white girls being deflowered. In other words, they wanted their big black bucks not to be too black.

Just black enough, one supposes, to fuck a white girl.

According to Pat Riley, a pornography expert who posts

rants and raves about the industry on his porn info site RAME (rame.net), "for the longest time,"

the porn industry ... [traded] in the most pejorative views of blacks it [could] find. Pornographers perpetuate the stereotypical view of a shiftless, maladjusted group. [Racism in porn] is not some white actress who doesn't want to screw a black guy (for whatever reason) but a concerted attempt by the producers to appeal to the basest elements of the viewing population.

But then there was the porn-era post–Sean Michaels, an articulate, bespectacled, briefcase-carrying black stud who played scenes as if he was a black Gregory Peck with a ten-inch dick running down the leg of his boxers underneath his gray flannel suit. Sean had single-handedly changed the rules for brothers in the porn game. Not only was he "palatable" but he was smarter than the average stud, more sophisticated than the average viewer, a tall ebony-skinned Adonis who never soiled his white collar.

"Sean paved the way for me," Steele told me. "All roads lead back to Sean Michaels and what he did for the image of the black guy in porn." Essentially Michaels had retrieved the tropes of standard white-boy professionalism and flipped it into a sort of sexy pose of black-boy cool. So you had to be just black enough (and hung big) to fuck a white girl, but not so threatening that you scare her in the parking lot after the shoot.

According to Steele, his video releases sell like, well, hot-cakes. Whereas most new porn videos will move approximately three thousand or so pieces upon initial release, then trail off at about five thousand copies over the next six months, Steele's titles such as *Heavy Metal, Volumes 1 and 2,* will move five thousand copies upon release. Others have moved up to seven thousand pieces upon release and move about ten thousand copies in the next three months. These are major numbers in the porn market. And at $12 a pop, that's quite a few coins for an entrepreneurial porn actor to jangle in his pocket.

Lexington Steele, college-educated former Wall Street broker, works in a business where strangers fuck strangers for money, where the big black beast is an accepted role to be played in a public space, for a huge fan base of black men who worship him as the sexual superhero that he portrays on-screen and white men who want to see Steele whipping out his big black monster dick and ferociously putting it to a tiny white girl. Steele feels the sexual sting of stereotyping every day he goes to work: as the hung black stud he's the personification of a stereotype that controls the very image of black men everywhere, yet he has to rely on the stereotype as a fantasy creation to ensure that he stays on top of his game. Steele laughs as he recounts this, mostly, it seems, because he realizes the utter paradox of it—culturally and economically speaking.

"By nature," Steele said, "this business isn't about any color except green—money. I mean, the only thing that separates it from being prostitution is that there's a camera in the room when people are doing their thing." As a producer, as someone who hires and fires talent every day, Steele has a fairly sanguine approach to it all, particularly coming up against the casting of white women and the usual conflicts that arise around that issue. "I don't have a problem with hiring white girls who want to work. I'm seeing product. My own films don't have a color line. All races are represented in the scenes. However if you allow my brown skin to overshadow my green money, then fuck you, that's your loss."

Not that this behavior is limited to the stars of the business. "I've met girls fresh off the bus from West Virginia or Utah, coming into this business and immediately stating that they don't do black guys. This from a girl who's probably fucked her way across the country to get here, who wants to make a living fucking strangers on camera. She'll fuck for money, but she won't do it with a black dude." He laughs off such a contradiction because he also knows there's a secret buried in that paradox—as there usually is when race and sex meet for a little session. "The thing is," he told me, "that many, many of these girls who 'won't screw a black guy' really mean that they won't screw a black guy *on-screen*. I know of a few of these women who do private shows with black guys. Let some rapper call, or some basketball player ring up and say he wants to get down. Then let's see these females talk about 'not screwing black guys.' "

"I take the good with the bad," he added. "Of course there're elements to doing this that doesn't necessarily add up. It can be both emasculating as well as empowering." Emasculating because "you know you're the animal phallus, the beast. I know that I'm dealt with for what's between my legs, but at the same time, there's something to being cherished, to being the desired one even as you know you're fill-ing a stereotype."

Said by the man who looked to the hip-hop music industry and World Wrestling Federation to find a way of crafting a branded image for himself. "You know how rappers and wrestlers are like characters?" he told me. "That's my model. Method Man can be Johnny Blaze or whoever else. I can be the Impaler, the Dark Prince, the Black Viking."

He's the guy who is the soft-spoken cat, opening the first installment of *Heavy Metal* by inviting a journalist into his home to interview him, then modestly pulling out his eleven-inch dick when she asks to see it, telling her that it's not even the biggest one in the porn biz. He's the guy who ends his time with me quoting Dr. Frances Cress Welsing, a noted the-orist on race. Welsing has a theory about color, about how it is color itself—before you even get to the invented tropes of stereotypes and myths—that intimidates people, that the sheer appearance of black or brown skin is the perceived opening salvo in the waged war of race hatred that has plagued human relations.

War, indeed. The first *Little White Chicks and Big Monster Dicks* (1999) opens with a disclaimer that the filmmaker (Jake Steed) doesn't mean to attack any racial group. But it cer-tainly can't be an accident that the director/producer of the video—billed as a Jake Steed Production—is credited as A. Trublackman. Jake Steed: a True Black Man, Who's Hung Like a Horse.

The black male body is, I've decided, something like American history's Trojan horse, hiding in plain sight, invisible as its real self yet highly visible as its mythical self, a hopefully benign gift unwrapped to expose a seething mass of warring contradictions, the enemy in the midst. Perhaps porn is the place that expresses this better than anything.

Maybe the phrase should be hung like a Trojan horse?

South Beach: A Fantasia

It was the fall of 2000, the autumn of our great new century, and I was feeling like I had to get the hell out of New York City. One month earlier, I'd been a very well compensated employee of a dot-com company attempting to construct an all-encompassing home on the Internet for primarily "urban" (read "of color") Webheads. The company's tagline, its clever claim to fame, was this: First Generation Urban. The company fancied itself a sort of savior to the urban Internet cause, housing numerous eclectic Web sites under one spiffy umbrella, its point of view ostensibly constructed to reflect the concerns and desires of all of us who'd moved past simple race identification toward a more inclusive "urban" experience. This was the future and the future was now.

I'd been a journalist and a talking head on TV. I'd made a name for myself. I was some sort of swinging dick. And I gave it all up to be a part of the new media future: I was an executive at a splashy dot-com company. At least until the bottom fell out. When the money was gone and the venture capitalists disappeared, I was something new: a laid-off victim of the dot-com boom, or, as I liked to tell people, officially a citizen of the twenty-first century. And when you're a recently laid-off employee of a splashy dot-com, well, you don't feel your dick swinging all that much.

It was around that time, jobless and with no leads and feeling like a fool, that I made a decision. I was going to give it *all* up and start from scratch. I wasn't going to be "urban," first generation or otherwise. I wasn't going to be part of the hip-hop generation. All the labels were going to be erased. I was going to leave New York City and find some fresh pasture to graze, some new field to plow. I wanted to go somewhere else, someplace where I could get out of myself, could watch instead of being watched, could listen without expecting necessarily to be heard, could hear music and not be compelled to dance as fast as I could.

So, like some kind of seasonal bird, I spread my wings and flew south, landing in south Florida.

Miami Beach is a crime scene waiting to happen. If you squint your eyes in the blazing sun you can almost see the yellow crime-scene tape that will eventually, inevitably surround everything around you. The first time I was down there, in that lush Latin city on the beach edge of the south Florida marshes, the mayor was arrested for throwing a teapot at his wife and spent a night in jail. A city official was arrested for exposing himself in the men's room of a public park. News was circulating of a spy ring, which meant that strangers at dinner parties and barbecues received clandestine, who-might-you-be stares. A tourist from New York was found in a suitcase floating near a yacht in Biscayne Bay, her arms and legs missing, her torso encased in a tight leather minidress.

You wake up in the morning and the early news is recounting an accidental drowning in an Olympic-sized pool that most likely wasn't accidental. You catch the midday newscast and the painfully blond newscaster with the pancake makeup is listing the names of teenagers collared by the cops as they exited the house they'd just robbed on Star Island.

Don't get me wrong. Miami is a beautiful city, a palm-tree-lined, tropical port of call, old and elegant, yet new and robust, energized by solar power like a sun-kissed plant growing awkwardly over the edges of its pot. Miami is like a sexy jaded tourist who attached herself to the American dream and decided to stay for a while. There's something damp and surreal about the beauty that is Miami, something fetid in the fluorescence, something wicked under the glamorous façade. New York is a hard city and Los Angeles is a plastic city and New Orleans is a careless city; Las Vegas has a slot machine where its heart should be and Chicago's big shoulders shrug to a rhythm that knows how to demand respect, but none of those totemic American cities has what Miami Beach has, which is an almost religious addiction to change. For all its feel of foreignness, it's very, postmodernly *American* in that way; Miami Beach might be the most American city of them all.

I met Nico in Miami. I was sitting at a diner on the corner of Eleventh Street and Washington, cutting into a stack of pancakes, when this guy sits down in the booth next to me and says, "I've seen you around and I think you must be from New York City."

"I've seen you around," I said back to him, "and you are right."

Nico proceeded to tell me about the long night he'd just en-
dured, which had begun at a dinner meeting with his "agent."
I put agent in quotes because when Nico told me about his
"agent" he put his hands in the air, one near each cheek, framing his mouth, and did that quotation mark thing that dramatic
people do. It seemed that Nico's "agent" was thinking of leav-
ing the "business"—more quotation marks from Nico—and
wanted to introduce Nico to a "manager" who he thought
could take Nico further in the "business." The "business" in
this case is the fashion business, an outpost of which gives
work to models and photographers and stylists in Miami
Beach, specifically in South Beach, where I sit, trying to eat
pancakes and watching Nico put almost every other word that
comes out of his mouth into quotation marks.

Nico was a model. He'd done some print work, he told me,
in New York, and he'd done some runway work in Los
Angeles, not to brag, because it's not like runway work in Los
Angeles is any great shakes in the "grand scheme of things."
The "grand scheme of things," I'd find out, was one of Nico's
phrases, something he said often to give dramatic emphasis to
a point he wanted to make. "In the grand scheme of things," he
told me that morning, "I don't even know if I'll need a manager." Then he said no more about his "agent" or his "manager" or the "business." He proceeded to ask questions about
me. What had brought me to Miami, to South Beach? What
was I running away from? "Because just about everybody in
Miami who ain't from Miami is here because they're running
away from something," he told me. He wanted to know all
about my life in Manhattan, who I knew that he might know,
where I shopped, what I drank and where I drank it.

It occurred to me, sitting there in that diner, the syrup around my pancakes congealing, that Nico might have been some kind of hustler, that he was trying to get as much information out of me as he could, to pull some kind of scam, maybe identity theft (something else I'd heard was happening all over Miami Beach) or some long con that required that he ingratiate himself to me. But my suspicions didn't stop me from continuing the conversation. Mostly because Nico was charming, and beautiful, and entertaining as hell, with his overblown mannerisms and "grand scheme of things." He stood about six feet, somewhere between one-seventy-five, one-eighty, and he was cut.

Imagine the statue of David dipped in a vat of caramel and chocolate and left to dry in the Miami Sun.

When I look over the diary I kept that first winter in South Beach, certain words jump out at me, particularly in relation to Nico. I see "sex" on almost every page, in almost every paragraph. Here's something Nico said about the ratio of fake breasts to real ones near the pool of the Delano Hotel. And here's something Nico told me about the first time he'd had sex with his girlfriend, how they were both drunk out of their heads and ready for anything. Nico told me about how he'd traded sex for "modeling" jobs while he'd been in Miami. And he told me about the "jobs" that only entailed sex, which came more often than the modeling jobs. He told me about these latter things because my initial reaction to him had been correct: Nico *was* a hustler. But not a confidence-scheme hustler, swindling innocent (and some not-so-innocent) folks out of their hard-earned money. Nico was in the sex game, the "pleasure zone" as he called it, trading sexual favors for money, mostly to men, mostly to vacationers, out-of-towners who flocked to Miami for some "fun in the sun," as Nico—and, I assumed, they—called it.

Once Nico showed me the ad he'd placed on the Internet, essentially an online profile describing himself and the acts he performed, the services he rendered, when the money was right. According to the ad, Nico was "6'/180, with hazel(ish) eyes and a big fat black dick." Since I was on the computer already, I sent Nico an instant message with the words "big fat black dick" in quotation marks with a "curious face" icon next to it. A few seconds later, he returned the message. He said, "Yes. Big fat black dick. What don't you understand about that?" "I understand that you're Latin," I wrote back. "So how can you have a 'big fat black dick'?" He returned an LOL—Internet-speak for "laugh out loud"—and said, "I'm only Latin when I want to be."

Later, over drinks, Nico explained to me that in his business, a big fat black dick is like money in the bank, a slam dunk, a sure thing. He explained to me that in the sex trade, Latin guys were popular but the guys he'd met who requested Latins were looking for Ricky Martin, not a beautiful dark-brown Cuban papi who didn't fit their fantasy. "You might meet some hick from Idaho who's never seen a Latin dude and wants something exotic for a night or a coupla hours, but for the most part, the people that I meet and the people that a lot of my boys meet want the fantasy of the big black dick."

I could only look at him. Which was fine with him. "I can pass for black," he said. "Latins are of African descent as well." But what Nico was selling, ultimately, was "African American." That was the fantasy. These guys wanted Mandingo. Besides, he added, "Once you tell them you're black, then you get there and whip out the big dick, they believe anything you tell them."

Nico's clients, for the most part, were white men—usually wealthy, cultured, educated men with wealthy, cultured, educated wives—who were away from their wives and looking for something that their wives obviously couldn't give them. He turned some tricks for white women, but most of the white women, he told me, had their husbands around, watching the action, as Nico serviced the wife. "Very *American Gigolo*," he told me. One couple, he said, both wanted to be serviced. "So I fucked 'em both up the ass," he said, sipping from his mojito. "That was a wild night."

"And you told them you were black?" I said, meaning African American.

"I told them I was black."

Nico was surprised by my open-mouthed shock that he was passing as a black guy to do this. It was clear to Nico that race and sex go hand in hand. That's not new. It's history. But he also realized it for the fantasy, the myth, that it was. These people have a fantasy that they need made into reality, like they need to believe that that big dick exists out there so they can have access to it. He sipped some more of his drink and told me, "One guy hired me and all he wanted to do was watch a football game and ask me questions about my dick, like how big was it when I was a kid, if my dad had a big dick or my brothers, when was the first time I'd measured it. Shit like that. Paid me for my time, didn't want to have sex, just wanted to look at it and talk. He'd look from my dick to the football game, then back to my dick again. Easy money. My big fat black dick."

In my journal notes from that time in Miami, "BFBD" is next to Nico's name on a few pages, where, apparently, I'd written it in the margins, mad to remember it.

It seemed odd to me, I told Nico, that in Miami Beach—that enclave of relocated Cubans and rich Colombians and transplanted Nuyoricans, that most Latin of American cities—that a dude like himself would need to pass as an African American to make his dime. "Look, in the grand scheme of things, what else would you do? Sure I could make money being 'Latin,' but why do that when the big money is in being black? It's all one big movie anyway. We're all playing a part in one big ole movie. If saying I'm black pays my rent and keeps me going to auditions and all that, you damn straight I'm gonna say I'm black since I'm hung like the black guy of their fantasies. If I wasn't hung like this, believe me, none of those white folks would believe it."

Hung like a black guy. I couldn't help thinking about the eracist guy Ty and his European girl. Was Nico an eracist too? Or just a cynic?

I told Nico about that quote from James Baldwin, that as far as white people went, as far as most people went, the color of the dick was the size of the dick. He thought about this for a little while, his chin in his hands, then nodded and said, "He's probably right. I have a buddy who's sorta hung—"

"What's 'sorta' hung?" I had to ask.

"He's about eight and a half, fully hard," said Nico. "And when he's fucking these white men they all tell him to work that big black dick, so, in the grand scheme of things, there you go."

"Eight and a half," I'd written in my journal. "That's *'sorta hung,'* according to Nico. Is that like being 'sorta pregnant' or 'sorta rich'?" I've known guys who flaunted their own eight and a half inches as being *really* hung, not *sorta* hung. If eight and a half inches is "sorta hung" what was nine inches? Ten inches? Was that what folks meant when they said "well hung"? Perhaps this was just a Miami thing, I thought. Everything in Miami is outsized and flamboyant, colorful and full of life. Drama is in the blood here, in this place of transplanted wannabe stars and model-hustlers masquerading, reverse-style, across the color line.

"Big dicks," says my friend Renee, "do not guarantee good sex."

Renee is a fashion stylist who works in Manhattan and Miami, pairing celebrities with the clothes that get them noticed on red carpets. She is, she likes to joke, the only celebrity stylist in the world with undergrad and advanced degrees from Ivy League universities. She is, she likes to tell me, the only celebrity stylist who thinks most celebrities are idiots, "walking advertisements for vacuousness," most of them "about as dumb as a bag of hair." She considers what she does modern-day anthropology, mining the fashion runways and designer showrooms she frequents as the caves where she finds the frocks that celebrities wear to make regular people feel bad about themselves.

Renee is, she likes to tell me, nobody's fool. Which is why

she so often finds herself resisting the constant invitations and old urges she has to sleep with any of the male celebrities—mainly athletes and rappers—she dresses for award shows and charity banquets. "You'd have to be a fool to deal with one of those guys," she told me that first winter in South Beach. "The best you can hope to get from any encounter with one of these guys is the most intense rush of self-loathing in the world."

Renee and I were talking about her decision not to date rappers and athletes because Nico had recounted for us, sitting on the purple sun-dappled porch of the Marlin Hotel on Collins Avenue, a story about the one athlete customer he "bottoms" for whenever they meet for a rendezvous. By "bottoming," Nico means being the receptive partner in their sexual escapades, the submissive to this athlete's dominant, the "girl," as the athlete likes to refer to him, to the athlete's "boy."

Nico would not tell us the name of this athlete; he would only tell us which sport the guy played and which city he played in. It only took a few more hints from Nico—the athlete's taste in underwear, his taste in women, his taste in expensive vodka—for Renee to blurt out the athlete's name.

Nico would neither confirm nor deny. He just continued with his story.

"So he goes on," Nico told us, "about how he wants to bring a coupla friends along the next time we do our thing. And I go, 'I don't think so.' There's not enough money in the world for me to bottom for all of them. And besides, I don't ride trains. What do I look like? Some kinda commuter? I don't even ride the subway when I'm in New York."

Renee finds this whole angle on the athlete interesting, because, she said, "He has a little dick."

"Why do you think I bottom for him? You think I'm taking major trade back there? I mean, I like to think of myself as versatile, but what do I look like? Some kind of dick hog? Not me."

"Major trade," I'd written in my journal from that winter in South Beach. I had to laugh rereading it, just as I had when I heard Nico say it on the porch of the Marlin Hotel. "Trade" had been a slang word for dick when I was just out of college in the late eighties, and probably popular slanguage long before that. It reminded me of gay guys, flamboyant dudes in riding boots and tight jeans sweating on the dance floors of New York nightclubs. It also reminded me of a novel I'd read in the eighties in which a teenage hustler was referred to as "trade," as in something for sale, for barter, like a piece of meat or clothing. I'd also heard that "trade" was a common word for a presumably straight guy getting serviced by a primarily gay guy, a straight boy who didn't cavort in the scene of New York nightclubs, yet found a way to trick sex out of a gay boy. "Trade of doom" is how I recalled a guy saying that a dude he'd slept with was hung big. "Massive trade," "major trade," "trade of life": all descriptive phrases to signify significant dick size, a phraseology as flamboyant and colorful as the house music and psychedelic shirts that defined gay urban life of the late eighties and early nineties.

Back in those days immediately after college, I danced until dawn in downtown nightclubs, hypnotized by the voguing queens on the dance floor and captivated by the carefree air of life hyper-lived to a sound track of disco divas and decadent

DJs. But I was also knee-deep in the hip-hop hoopla of the music biz, a sort of square suburban kid looking for hipness in the lingo of rappers destined to drop science, as we called it then, on how we lived on that edge of the world called black boyhood. I'd encountered several of those "walking adver-tisements for vacuousness" along the way, which Renee, as my close friend, knew about, and that was how I insinuated myself back into the conversation on the sun-dappled porch of the Marlin Hotel that day.

Nico didn't look surprised at the wide range of my youth-ful sexual experiences. He merely nodded and said, "Then you know what I'm talking about. You probably weren't fuckin' around with no major trade either." Then he turned to Renee and asked, "So how do you know my boy has a little dick?"

"I dressed him once and he took off his underwear right in front of me like he was doing me some kind of favor. But think about it, doesn't he act like he has a little dick? You know how some guys just *seem* like they aren't packing any-thing down there? Some guys just don't have the swagger that comes with having a big dick. I knew before he even disrobed in front of me that there wouldn't be a hell of a lot of stuff to write home about."

Nico agreed with Renee about the idea of "swagger" that comes with being more studly than other guys. I told them that I'd heard other women say that.

"Women know," Renee said. "You can tell from how a guy approaches you or even how he approaches the world. If he's packing between his legs, there's a sort of glide to his step, like an ownership of his surroundings. Athletes can fake you out though. They're so in control of their bodies that you can sometimes mistake that for hangature."

I said to Renee that I thought she didn't sleep with athletes.

"That doesn't mean," she said, "that I didn't at one time."

So I asked her if she looked for a big dick when she looked for a sex partner.

She nodded. "But mainly in the metaphorical sense of a big dick," she said. "Meaning if I feel like you can toss me around and get me off, the size of your dick doesn't really matter. Just take control and make me feel it. A literal 'big dick' is nice to look at and all, but a dick is really just a tool. It's only one part of the package that you bring to the table. A lot of guys think if they slow-drag with you on the dance floor and get hard and press that slab of meat against you, wham bam, they got you—signed, sealed, and delivered. But those are also, more often than not, the guys that coast by on that big-dick thing, like all they have to do is zip down that zipper, flop this big dick in your face, and expect you to worship it and do all the work for them to get off."

"You sound like a lesbian," Nico said.

Renee shook her head. "I'm not saying that I don't like a big dick, I'm just saying that I don't know if I like the attitude that comes with it. You know what big-dick privilege is like? It's like white-girl privilege. You know how you see a white girl at the store and she acts like she can step in front of you at the counter and she's swinging her hair around and sighing and acting like somebody needs to notice how much of a white girl she is? That's how dudes with gigantic dicks act. Like, will you stop kissing my chest and just worship my dick already?"

"That kind of attitude keeps me in Prada shoes," said Nico.

"If we're talking physically," said Renee, "I will say that there is something to be said for a guy going deeper inside you and filling up more space. It feels a little more sensitive, like there's more penetration. That can be hot. But if you have a big dick and you have that confidence *without* the attitude? That is *real* hot. If you have that big dick you might be more confident about the job you're doing and with confidence a guy will be a better lover."

"I agree," Nico said. "Because ain't nobody turned on by the humble guy coming off like the 'little dick' dude. That ain't gonna make you come."

Listening to their descriptions of confidence, to Renee's differentiation between literal big dick-ness and metaphorical big dick-ness, I thought of my friend Simon, whom Renee also knew. I described Simon to Nico: his suburban upbringing, his successful professional life, his desire to transcend race rather than be defined by it, and the way he'd experienced his reputation for literal big dick-ness, the way he felt it had defined him in the world as a black man, how it had positioned him to be judged and vilified.

"It didn't stop him from sleeping with all those white girls," huffed Renee, lighting a cigarette, the haze of smoke surrounding her face like a memory of our drunk and smoky college days.

"You know what it sounds like his problem is?" Nico said. "Sounds like he got the big dick but he ain't got the swagger to go with it. As far as I'm concerned, it ain't worth meeting a guy with a big dick if he ain't got the balls to prop it up."

When I look back over those journal notes from that period in South Beach, I see that so many of my dreams were sexual in nature, like elegant, sepia-toned porno films starring people I knew in my waking hours. This, of course, had to be because of Nico and his need to tell me as much of his personal business as he could muster, usually when we were drunk on cocktails in the lounge of some Collins Avenue hotel. Maybe I was meant to meet Nico when I got to Florida, since I'd figured out that *something* had brought me to South Beach. Maybe I needed to be in a place of crime and sex and scandal that was like New York but heightened a step and colorized like an old MGM film. I see that I'd written at the start of my third week there that "Miami not only clings to 'change' but it cleaves itself to sex. This city is positively ripe."

And I knew this wasn't only because of Nico and his tales of tricks and treats. There are descriptions in my journal of a roving pack of four beautiful shirtless white boys, their skin recently bronzed by the south Florida sun, and the one beautiful black girl who seemed to always be with them. I'd first noticed this pack of lithe lookers loitering on the corner of Eleventh and Collins, outside the bodega where I bought my cigarettes, the only bodega that sold my cigarettes in a fresh and smokable state, next door to the café where the most luscious Cuban girl in the world sold me Cuban coffee every morning. The pack of four white guys and one black girl, who I think was dating one of the guys, stood around that morning, every pair of eyes in every head of their group looking spooked to be witnessing an hour before noon. They lingered, chatting quietly, then headed west toward Ocean Drive, toward the beach, slouching in that way that only beautiful people can slouch, with the knowledge that good posture is for those less fortunate in the looks department. I saw them again the next day, on the mall-ish length of Lincoln Road, huddled outside Books and Books, still slouching but smiling, their eyes less shocked by the sunlight but probably only because they were drooped with the heavy aftereffect leer of some very good weed. I saw them later that night, still on Lincoln Road, as I sat outside a Cuban Chinese restaurant sipping a German lager that felt too heavy for South Beach yet was perfect because it tasted just like the ambivalence that had brought me there from New York in the first place. Every time I saw this little crew, the black girl, her hair a mass of curls flowing down her back, was wearing a bikini top, her smooth abdomen a testament to youth and possibility, a tiny and taut expanse brushed with a brownness that could only symbolize an invitation to paint a bright and wild future. They were always laughing, this crew of friends, and in my journal I wrote that "they were like lit candles waiting to be blown (out?), inviting you to make a wish on the off chance that you had the power to blow them." Was I regressing to that sexually experimental state I'd experienced in the late eighties and early nineties, when I was young and hitting the streets, my mind lubed with weed and the possibility of sex? I couldn't have, because as beautiful as the white boys were, caught somewhere in a nexus of Abercrombie and Fitch homoerotic clone-dom and Just Do It jockitude, they weren't as interesting to me as they might have been back in my college days, when the idea of conquering some pretty white dude played itself out in a myriad of self-defeating ways.

No, this was all about the cinnamon-brown sista who led them around town on some invisible leash of desire. I took to calling her Diana in my mind and in my journal because of the Diana Ross hair that flowed behind her. Diana became a talisman of sorts, redolent of sex and fun in the sun and the glory of being desired.

Perhaps I'd allowed these kids to exist fantastically in my imagination because I didn't feel all that desirable myself, as invisible as I'd made myself in Miami. I'd spent so much time there revisiting my past, recent and ancient, that I'd ceased to exist in any present tense. And I was beginning to wonder if I'd made the right decision to drop it all and escape. There'd been hard times before, very vivid memories of not feeling particularly well hung even when I'd been told that I was a success story who did, symbolically, measure up. I had my laundry list of accomplishments and published articles brandishing my byline. I'd been the accomplished black man in the white man's world; I'd been a Solo Negro and a first black; I'd seen the promised land that isn't promised to a man-child like me and I'd learned that as quickly as it can come, it could be pulled away from you.

I remembered that back in the day, when I'd first gotten to NYC and started that march up the ladder, a friend suggested that we do a book called *How I Got Over,* which would outline all the ways for high-minded ambitious cats like us to cut corners, learn the rules and sometimes break them, and, ultimately, play the games the way they needed to be played. Of course we could write that book: we were destiny's children, long before Beyoncé and her crew stole our name and blew up the spot. The spot was ours to be blown. All we had to do was make sure we had the dynamite to make it happen. And now here I was, in the mutable, sexually charged land of South Beach, the diamond in the tiara of Dade County, sipping a German lager and creating symbolic fantasies about a college girl not named Diana and her crew of beautiful white guys like they were mythical creatures, like they could somehow make me feel better about myself.

Then again, I came to realize, isn't that what symbolic fantasies are for, isn't that what myths do: make one feel better about one's own condition?

The last time I saw Diana and her crew, they were across the street from my apartment, checking out of a hotel and lugging suitcases into a blue-and-yellow airport shuttle van. Each and every one of them wore a T-shirt with the word "Brown" emblazoned across the front. How delicious was this? And prescient? Diana and her crew were spring breakers. Of course they were, traveling in that protective little group as they did, high on weed and life and sun and the rhythms of their own fabulousness. And they were students at my old college. Imagine that. Had I sensed that somehow? Or was this some kind of sign? Was I supposed to read some sort of message in this?

I left Miami early the next year. I returned to New York City and started writing again. I lost touch with Nico. I think about him often and I smile. Even if his paid public persona was a lie, I thought his forthright sexuality, his go-for-broke passion, was completely for real.

These days when I read my notes from those months in South Beach, I'm not embarrassed to say that I sometimes get an erection. I might have felt dead when I went down there, but I came back to life.

New Directions: Hip-Hop Hooray

Music helped bring me back to life. When I'd left for Miami, I'd also been in a very anti-hip-hop mode. Wasn't listening to it and, other than the Eminem and Missy Elliott profiles I did for *The Source,* wasn't writing about it either. Mainly because there wasn't much that was interesting to me in the music that had, for the most part, defined my teenage years. And when the white boy from Detroit and the woman from Virginia were the only rappers I felt compelled to even think about— were, in fact, the rappers whose stories I wanted to hear—I knew there was something wrong.

The story of black men is one about storytelling. And as Joan Didion reminded us in *The White Album,* we tell ourselves stories in order to live. We find narratives that explain what we see and how we see it, what we hear, what we do, what we know and how we know it, deciphering codes and uncovering symbols, looking for the thread of facts that floss the gears, keeping the machinery of our lives running smoothly, elegantly.

Elegance, however, is something Americans have never

really known: we know how to pretend we have some strong and definite ties to politeness and subtlety, to beauty and correctness. But we don't. We float between these two oceans, rocking and rolling with the currents, wondering if the waves will ever wash over us and put out the flames of what James Baldwin called "this burning house of ours."

Here's a story.

In one of the rooms of this burning house, downstairs somewhere in a basement we rarely rifle through, some black kids got together and, bored with the plain ole funky drumming of their parents' records, plowed the vinyl for beats, scratching the platters back and forth, finding combustible new grooves. Over these popping, itching sounds, kids made up rhymes, battling their ghetto brethren with witty, raunchy tales of life and love and ego. Soon these new sounds were given a name, rap music, and they found their own way onto a vinyl of its own, sold out of mom-and-pop shops near the liquor stores on inner-city corners. Soon they found their way into the ears of white folks who came to see what all the ruckus was about. Soon the rhymers started rhyming less about life and love and ego and more about the problems plaguing the pursuit of life and love and ego. Soon they were declaring in broad strokes that even if you couldn't smell the smoke in your part of the house, the house was indeed on fire, and after years of watching older black folks narrowly survive the flames at their coattails, the rhymers didn't give a fuck: in a world where selling drugs and gangbanging and cruising around in hyped-up rides became the cool pose of inner-city community living, only the government-sanctioned gang-bangers known as cops could really stop the ride.

Soon these new sounds were a marketable franchise, making some ghetto children rich beyond their expectations, making white folks richer, making a nation sit up and take notice of its rhythmic, resistant power—that is, when it didn't devolve into a fantasy-fulfilling theme-park ride of poor powerless black kids who were pretending to be rich and powerful for the ears of rich powerful white kids who were pretending to be poor and powerless. Let's sing it all together: "The roof . . . the roof . . . the roof . . . the roof is on fire. We don't need no water, let the motherfucker burn."

Boy oh boy oh boy.

Boy, indeed: B-boy to be precise. The rise of hip-hop signaled the official cultural arrival of the B-boy, the block boy, the ghetto warrior speaking truth from the front. This was also boy love, posse power, an encoded and fetishized way for black men to rise up and regale the world with information that, it seemed, only they could impart.

But it's a provocative course to travel from "boy" because, unless it has that aggressive extra "B" in front of it, "boy" is a word that black men don't take too kindly to. One of those history-charged linguistic phenomena that Americans know so well, "boy" bespeaks a legacy of forced underachievement, thwarted goals, misplaced history—or, simply, a presupposed lack. In the age of hip-hop, a postwar cultural product just as reliant on the arrogance of youth as rock and roll, however, "boy" was recaptured (sort of like, ahem, "nigga") and found a new corporate life, but with a twist: youth was truly hipness, hipness was truly blackness, so who better to set the standard for savage cultural chicness than black boys from the 'hood?

Only, these boys were great pretenders; the boys from

around the way couldn't just be boys. A new world order of inner-city chaos and suburban angst made them men before they were supposed to be—or at least they acted like it did—resulting in a sort of cultural priapism, building myths of hardness, of coolness. We couldn't be the smartest and we wouldn't be the richest (though we'd die trying to attain status as the latter), we were told, but we could be the baddest—and rebuild the black boy as a public spectacle of cool, against the heat-releasing background of the burning house we called home.

No doubt boyhood—new and fresh, eager to make a mark—is where mythmaking begins. With hip-hop there were new myths being created, as myths tend to be, from the detritus of other myths, myths that black men over the years had both relished when celebrated for them and resisted when chafed by them.

Because hip-hop was a new era of black male invention, the creation of a new disguise for brothers to don, pieced together from the remnants of all sorts of fabrics, I've always thought of hip-hop as a way that black men snatched back their masculinity from the clutches of crossover culture. Before the true hip-hop explosion, black music in the eighties was represented by a string of mellow singer dudes who, while immensely talented, maintained an air of unthreatening appeal to the masses, from Lionel Richie to Freddie Jackson. Smooth crooners ruled the roost. And both Michael Jackson and Prince trafficked in a mascaraed androgyny that fit right into the times—Prince, of course, making a bold sexual statement in his tight pants and snarlingly phallic guitar slinging.

But the image of rappers seemed to have been crafted from

some combination of inner-city Black Power politics and the cinematic ballsiness of blaxploitation flicks. Rap music had an urban crotch-grabbing swagger that seemed to emphasize, with its bragging lyrics and street-smart vitality, the very defiant maleness of its performers. But for a long time, I found it curious that for all its very obvious boy love, its self-reflectively homosocial fetishization of all things male and ghetto and cool, hip-hop was so defiantly unsexy. Here was the original site of thug love, this rhythmic updating of the alluring American outlaw, courting attention to itself with a swagger and self-confidence. Yet for all that—except for maybe Big Daddy Kane, L.L. Cool J, and a couple others who fancied themselves "lover men"—rap was almost pathologically resistant to objectification, like the sexiest boy in class who was also the shyest. There were artists like Kool G Rap who rapped some real down-and-dirty ditties that dripped sex but for the most part even the sexual bragging took a backseat to metaphors that emphasized strength, savvy, general around-the-way superiority.

Then something happened. Hip-hop made its way from ghetto music of the black inner-city masses to well-hung crossover sensation. I think those two things happened because of L.L. Cool J's burgeoning fame and the discovery of Marky Mark.

Other rappers had appeared shirtless in videos, but none of them captured the public imagination like L.L. Cool J. James Todd Smith named himself Ladies Love Cool James, developing his own niche in the rap field by managing to be hardcore in the rhyme-skills department, yet still being secure enough to show his vulnerable side in love songs like "I Need Love." In his video for "I'm Bad," centered on the rescue attempt of his lady love, he went shirtless, flexing his muscles like the bastard child of an action star and a porn king. It was risky business for a rapper, but it worked for him.

By the time of his multi-platinum hit *Mama Said Knock You Out,* L.L. Cool J was a full-fledged sex symbol, dancing with girls in one video, appearing naked and glistening from the waist up on the album cover. But this had come after he'd gone through a period of criticism from the rap community because of his previous album, *Walking with a Panther.* That record had featured L.L. Cool J in full playboy mode—smack dab in the middle of rap's burgeoning Black Power era of Public Enemy and Poor Righteous Teachers—cavorting with models, toasting with champagne, blinging out before bling was either a noun or a verb that rappers even thought about using. Somehow what L.L. Cool J was doing at that moment was trivial and self-serving. It was selling sex when black men were supposed to be selling politics.

L.L. Cool J had no problem with being admired or desired for his perceived sexual prowess and charisma. It was almost as if he'd noticed the void in the public imagination of the sexual black stud and stepped right into it, making it his own, resisting two traditional tropes of rap music: he seemed to like women, never trading in the bitch/ho school of female name-calling, and he seemed to like sex.

For all of hip-hop's swagger, it did always seem to resist American culture's way of sexualizing black men. But the question of why loomed large. Was rap's tough-guy pose a way to stave off the stereotypical sex appeal of black men? Or did hip-hop just not care about those things? Had violence simply trumped sex as the main cliché of cultural pathology that was always hung onto rap music as a way of explaining its appeal? Was crotch-grabbing really just a way for rappers, even unconsciously, to hide their dicks, to avoid the eventual emasculation and/or demonization that seemed to threaten black men in the public eye?

Perhaps it was some sort of collective cultural consciousness dating back before the Black Power sixties and seventies, dating back to Jim Crow, that kept the black B-boy's body under wraps, to avoid the larger culture's exploiting it. Perhaps rappers were like my friend Simon, who felt as if he were "on show" because of his massive endowment. Perhaps rap music had reclaimed power over the black male body by, visually at least, not putting our business in the street.

I began to suspect that the lack of sex in rap music was about vulnerability. By the time of rap's rise from local Bronx sound track, the battle-scarred collective consciousness of young black folks, especially young black men, had made for a galvanized self-protective nature that didn't leave room for any vulnerability, for any hint of "softness." Rappers had taken the pro-black, edgy attitude of blaxploitation but they'd left the well-hung lover-man sex stud on the cutting-room floor.

I wrote a profile of L.L. Cool J for *Spin* magazine in 1991, upon the release of *Mama Said Knock You Out,* and the criticism I received for it only reconfirmed for me the notion that rap music wasn't interested in making sex and sexuality an issue. I spent days on the road with L.L. Cool J, from his tour rehearsals to the actual tour itself, at parties, at home, building a rounded sense of the man for a profile that I hoped would show the world another side of the rapper, the "hardest-working hard rock in the business" I called him. I didn't want a fluff piece on the man and his millions. I didn't want a treatise on life in the 'hood from the point of view of someone who'd made it out. No. I wanted to profile the artist, the egoist, the flawed man who could make minutes-old rhymes sound like age-old philosophy. I wanted to interview the sexy brotha from around the way who used sexuality to make artistic points. I wanted to get at the glittering charisma that made him as interesting a subject as Mick Jagger in his rock-star heyday.

And I did. There were my words, next to the dazzling Anton Corbijn photographs of the star at work and play, getting quotes from L.L. Cool J you'd never heard slip from the lips of a rapper, about ambition, about sex, about music, about life. And the only reason for that was: no one, it seemed, had ever asked him.

A funny thing happened on the way to my journalism revolution: a writer friend called and told me that I couldn't write about hip-hop and rappers the way I'd written about L.L. Cool J. What did he mean, the way I'd written about L.L. Cool J? I asked him, knowing full well what he was about to tell me. You can't write about rappers as sexual beings, he told me. You can't ask rappers about Madonna and pop culture, he said. You can only represent young black men as the warriors that they are.

I tried to explain that I wanted to investigate the sources of that "menace" Baldwin referred to when talking about "American masculinity"—I was twenty-three, I thought I knew everything. All it took, in my opinion, was to look at rap videos and listen to rap lyrics to know that this investigation was at the heart of much of the music. How do I become a man when the world thinks of me as a boy? How do I negotiate success when the world only wants to give me struggle? And along with all that, L.L. Cool J *was* a sex symbol. As funny as his lyrics were, as funky as his beats were, there was no denying that part of his appeal was his dimpled grin and bare-chested bravado, demonstrated to such great effect in his videos and exposed as his ticket to major-league stardom with the sepia-toned image of his *Mama Said Knock You Out* CD cover.

My friend wasn't buying it.

Then Calvin Klein happened to rap culture. And everyone started to buy it.

Before he was known as respected actor Mark Wahlberg, he was known as Marky Mark—thuggish little brother of a New Kid on the Block—who rapped rhymes as the leader of the Funky Bunch. To some extent his whiteness and debatable rhyming skills cost him a certain amount of street credibility with the hardcore rap audience, but he was a certified star in the early nineties, a definite fixture on MTV. When fashion designer Calvin Klein made him a bare-chested poster boy for his burgeoning underwear line, however, Marky Mark became an icon. Before Mark, Calvin Klein had always trafficked in a certain slick and upscale louche-ness in his ad campaigns, courting public debate and titillation to keep the word out about his products. He'd even been one of the first designers to fetishize the male body for public consumption, playing to fashion's already homoerotic image and breaking barriers around the issue of demonstrations of public desire. Klein recontextualized what it meant to be young, male, and sexy.

What he hadn't done, before Marky Mark at least, was be so forthrightly "street" in his approach.

But now, for an underwear ad campaign, Klein was wrapping his style around the smooth cut musculature of a rapper, which up to this point—1991, 1992—had meant L.L. Cool J. But overnight, it seemed, the predominant visual representation of the snarling face and crotch-grabbing street-tough urban warrior wasn't a black boy from the 'hood. The stud in this ad was Marky Mark, a white kid, grinning from ear to ear, the bottom half of his musculature clad in skintight underwear. Madison Avenue had never seen such an outright blend of hip-hop street appeal with overt preening male sexuality. Hip-hop had found its sexy-boy savior—and he was an Irish kid from Boston.

I remember seeing the first Marky Mark ad and thinking, "Wait, shouldn't that be L.L. Cool J up there, grabbing his crotch and flashing his pecs? Wasn't that *his* shtick?" Of course it was, but this was also Calvin Klein, never one to use too many black faces in his ad campaigns. This seemed to me to be the height of commercial eracism—sure, pop music had always stolen from black culture to beef up its own status and sound, but this was, it seemed, a fashion first. Klein, it seemed, wanted the "edge" of rap music, the crotch-first nasty street appeal of it, but not the color of it.

Before Calvin Klein's Marky Mark ad campaign rappers shied away from making the sexy black male body into a public spectacle. But hip-hop is nothing if not cynical about its power as a money-making force. And Marky Mark's rising star prompted the brothers to understand the growing acceptance of the male body as a site of public desire.

Heck, even Big Daddy Kane posed nude for *Playgirl.*

And as smooth rhythm and blues began to infiltrate the rap tracks, the shift toward letting a lot (if not all) of it hang out was nearing completion. Rappers started to understand that sex does indeed sell. Snoop Doggy Dogg wasn't just a weed-smoking ex-gangbanger from Long Beach. He was a lover, too. And you better act like you know. Several rappers were revealing their positions as porn connoisseurs, and some even became producers of porn, scoring the sex scenes to their own beats and rhymes.

Nowadays, listening to some rap tracks is like watching a porn movie in one's mind. The usual boasting and bragging that marked rap music as a black man's place for brothers to get the upper hand has given way to a graphic sexual sensibility that fits right in to the current cultural fascination with sex and sexuality. I think the floodgates opened with Lil' Kim's 1997 declaration that she "used to be scared of the dick" but could take it like a champ. Kim, in essence, gave brothers carte blanche to join the sexual fray and invite listeners into their own graphic sexual fantasies and scenarios. There's no room for the simple bragging metaphor for dick size or sexual ability.

50 Cent (with Lil' Kim) has built an entire song around the effects of his "Magic Stick." Ludacris gives advice to his fel-

low playas with lines like, "Know how to mack a broad, she's on your sack and balls / You call her Jabberjaws," on the cut "Splash Waterfalls." The gangster these days is also a lover, a pimp daddy as savvy at gatting an enemy as he is dicking down his female.

Yet as fraught as hip-hop can be with misguided, oversimplified cultural stereotypes of black male behavior, I've often sought to find something liberating in it, something defining about the community that's constantly reinventing itself to find a toehold in society. Hip-hop has never been a cultural phenomenon to me; it just *was*. It was the music of my northeastern U.S.-based youth, the sound of young America when I was a black boy growing up in the seventies and eighties. Hip-hop was my generation's representation of the hung, strong, young virile black male, taking no shorts, demanding respect. The tension for me personally was to find a way to dance to and celebrate a musical culture that seemed to cherish its limitations and boundaries as much as it celebrated its expansive musical palette.

For someone like me, living near the Color Line and considering himself sexually expansive, hip-hop could be a frustratingly limited entity. As much as I wanted to grab my crotch and proclaim my masculinity to the beat of a Bomb Squad–produced track, I needed to reconcile the fact that rap music was nonetheless as resistant to my sexual expansiveness as it was to sex in its early incarnations. And I had to reconcile myself to the fact that its resistance was partnered with a streak of violence toward and disdain for *anything* soft or feminine or even, it turned out, female. There was, it seemed, no space for women in rap—until there was. And there was little space for the sensitive boy. And thus there was, and still is, no space for the gay boy.

Little did one know that it would be the ever-expanding influence of hip-hop culture that would come to define, at the turn of the century, the very way many sexually suspect black men came to regard their sexual selves.

"Are you watching this?"

I'd answered the telephone to that starkly put question from my friend Maurice. "Am I watching what?" I asked him.

He was watching a show on HBO and they were doing a story about Roy Simmons, the first black NFL player to come out of the closet, post-career, as a gay man. Apparently, according to Maurice, Simmons was also HIV positive, which was part of the story. But the real story, it seemed, was how Simmons had lived his life "on the DL" before coming out. DL meaning "down low."

Congratulations, DL, you've made it to cable TV.

In 1992, a writing partner and I completed a screenplay about the hip-hop industry that prominently featured, among other characters, a gay rapper. Everyone who read it loved it. No one would buy it or produce it. ("This is a fairy tale," one producer told me, all puns intended.)

With the rise of the homo thug (more on him in a bit), we had a good story to tell, something that would comment on hip-hop's übermasculine posing. We both thought that having a character who was the best rapper in the story but who was also dealing with issues of sexual self-identity in a business made up of pseudonyms and concocted "keeping it realisms" would be something worth commenting about. But no one, we were told over and over, would believe it. The idea of a gay rapper, in the closet or otherwise, just wouldn't play.

This was before you could turn on the radio and hear murmured insinuations about the sex lives of rappers, before urban radio became a gossip mill devoted to the undercover goings-on of the hip-hop community. Times have most decidedly changed.

With this sudden rise in hip-hop sex appeal came something new: the gay rapper. Which, perhaps, should have been expected. I mean, with rappers starring in movies and TV shows, with their records going multi-platinum, with urban culture primarily mainstream youth culture, rappers are the newest breed of celebrity. And with celebrity—dating back to everyone from Marlon Brando and Montgomery Clift through Tom Cruise and Keanu Reeves—comes the inevitable question about sexuality. And all over urban radio, there it was: talk of the Gay Rapper.

For a long time, the Gay Rapper was some sort of free-floating myth. No one believed he existed and yet *everyone* did. He couldn't *really* exist because like priests, athletes, frat boys, and black men in general, a rapper couldn't be gay. "Gay" is the lowest form of insult one dude could hurl at another. And besides, the notion of a gay rapper wouldn't fit with the hardcore street-legal image. How could some dude strut across the video terrain with an Uzi and a video ho and be a fag? Rappers were going on the radio to deny that they were him, the Gay Rapper. Rappers were denying it in the press.

But the rumor stuck around. Probably, as most rumors do, because it was true.

For all it's gay-baiting nastiness, the talk about the Gay Rapper did force a question: Why couldn't a rapper be gay? The hip-hop game was all image anyway and you heard this same kind of stuff about stars in Hollywood. We knew there'd never be a rap version of, say, Rupert Everett or Boy George, someone out and proud and living his life. And we knew it because, in the black community at least, a secret had finally been revealed: the crime wasn't necessarily to be gay, the crime was to claim it.

Anyone who went to church in the 'hood every Sunday knew that as a truism. Sure, some dudes got with other dudes. But it was only done behind closed doors, in the closet. Which meant that there could very well be a rap version of Rock Hudson, living his life on the down low.

I'd met my share of closeted guys over the years. My college campus, like many, was rife with them. In my more politically minded collegiate years, I'd thought the closet was an evil thing, a place full of self-hating cowards too afraid to be themselves. Later I eventually accepted it as a choice, as part of a complex and complicated negotiation a guy had to make within himself to decide how he wanted to live his life. For all my early sissy-boy sensitivity, I think I was too hip-hop for the closet; either that or I just had a big mouth and didn't care what anyone thought of the choices I made about how to live my life. I also developed an aversion to labels: "gay" didn't mean what I needed it to mean for my own sexual experience and yet neither did "bisexual."

That was in the eighties, when calling oneself gay, particularly in a world defined by AIDS, was a loaded political choice, particularly for a black boy from a black family and an overwhelmingly conservative black community where homosexuality is seen as a white phenomenon, a sin, something shameful enough to be kept in the closet. Again, the crime would be to claim it, another unfortunate example of how shame defines the contradictory ways the black community often eshews any open discussion of sexuality.

The stereotypes work best: men are hung studs who only fuck women and women desire them. To be gay is, essentially, to be dickless, emasculated, and thus it is impossible to be the black man the community needs you to be. That was the message you received as a young black man; that was the message of hip-hop.

But somewhere in the rise of hip-hop, even guys who liked guys began to eschew the trappings of what it meant to be gay. As usual with young black men, they found an alternative way to express how they defined themselves and how they defined desire—or, at least, the presentation of it. Somewhere in the rise of hip-hop, guys who liked guys decided that butch was best, that the sissy had no place in the gay scheme of things. Somewhere in the rise of hip-hop, even the guys who liked guys realized that the thug got the love. This wasn't just about sexual roles—tops and bottoms, fuckers and fuckees—this was about the actual presentation of young black male masculinity.

The Homo Thug was born.

What exactly is a Homo Thug? On one level, the Homo Thug is the gay or bisexual black dude who has no problem reconciling his homo-ness with his hip-hop-ness. Or as one gay rapper told me once, with an odd mix of rapper bravado and gay-boy nonchalance: "I represent the new breed of homosexuals. We ain't drag queens or ultra-flamboyant. We blend. These are the niggas riding the A train and doing real things with real niggas." The Homo Thug is the eventual outgrowth of Banjy Realness, the category of gay voguing balls in which gay guys worked the runway in their best imitation straight boy.

I once wrote an article for *The Village Voice* about rap music videos and I called hip-hop "the longest walk for Banjy Realness there was," because, in my mind, there wasn't much difference between the real rappers and the gay boys who walked Banjy categories in the balls: both were playing dress-up to make a point and often could be indistinguishable from one another. Of course, it could be argued that my statement emasculated the rapper while it added a couple of inches to the gay boy—and, believe me, it did—but as far as I was concerned, it was the truth because at the end of the day, blending in was the natural order for black men living across sexual, economic, and political lines. And it never hurt to be thought of as masculine, as strong, as virile, as, ultimately, well hung.

The Homo Thug to me is the post–E. Lynn Harris generation of black gay boys; the gay house ball's "Walk for Banjy Realness" has come home to roost. As hip-hop mutates from its origins as well-hung theme music of the ghetto black masses, its strangle on the tropes of (straight) black masculinity (read: sexuality) has become a little more fluid and gay boys have known it all the time. These are dudes for whom the political notions of gayness aren't adequate to their self-expression: politically speaking, these boys aren't Act(ing) Up and there's not much time for subversive or defiant queenisms. Fitting in is their rebellious way of standing out.

Unfortunately, it's also a way of hiding out. Because the Homo Thug very often is a guy on the down low.

An acquaintance of mine I'll call Darren is a Homo Thug. And he is a rapper. Talking to Darren about his sexual lifestyle is always an experience. He talks about his girlfriend Keisha in the most reverent of tones. He talks about his male lover Gregory in the most tender of tones. They each, according to Darren, satisfy different parts of who he is. He can dominate Keisha and he can be dominated by Gregory. And since he's never going to be with Gregory in any real, relationship way, it's not important that Keisha ever find out about him. But even more than Keisha, to Darren it's important that no one "around the way" finds out about his sexual activity with Gregory. "It'll make me seem like less a man," he tells me.

"In whose eyes?" I ask him.

"The peeps."

Though it's clear to me while talking to Darren that it's not just "the peeps" who really bother him. It's his own reflection staring back at him from the mirror he spends so much time looking in. Darren believes that to openly describe himself as gay would be to lower himself to a level where he doesn't think he deserves to be. To openly live a life that includes sex with men would mean that he's weak, less a man.

I say to Darren, "Did you ever think that perhaps your life isn't really yours?"

No, he tells me, that's never occurred to him.

But the next time we're chilling he tells me that his life *isn't* his own. His life is dictated by the forces of too many other things. By public opinion. By his family's possible revocation of their love for him. By the look that he can envision in his son's eyes if his son knew that he liked to suck dick.

"Your son will look at you like a man if you portray yourself that way to him," I tell Darren. "Your masculinity has absolutely nothing to do with who you have sex with."

Darren only gives me a shrug. I know he won't change. He knows it, too.

What up, pa!?!?! 5'9/160 22yo chocolate brown nikka on the DL, in dem Tims N sh*t, checkin for dem big-dick THUG nikkas on the DL . . . U know Who U B . . . If girls think U fine, U cool wid me . . . If nikkas clock U on the block, U ain't cool wid me . . . Bottom nikka here 4 THUG nikkas packin at least 8 . . . I keepz it real . . . pics in profile.

That is the Internet profile for "THUG4DK," a Homo Thug looking for sex. I always have to laugh when I read profiles like that one because: a) as direct and specific as the language is, it always seems so over the top; b) of how often the profiles that claim to be from a guy on the DL or a guy looking for a guy on the DL demand that the guy he's searching for is hung, which, in context, means defiantly that the guy should be more masculine than the next guy, more man than the next guy; and

c) the last line: pics in profile. It always occurs to me that if one is truly on the DL, one isn't putting one's pictures on the Internet for the world to see. What I had to learn was that THUG4DK probably, actually, isn't on the DL. "The DL" has sort of become a Homo Thug catchall meaning "not really all that gay" or, the one that gets me, "straight-acting." It means that THUG4DK locates his own desire in a thoroughly street, evidently hip-hop context. I love that THUG4DK and guys like him know exactly what they want and exactly how they want it. I love how the language, as over the top as it is, strives for a paradigm of hypermasculinity—"If girls think U fine, U cool wid me"—that is so desirable that it must be heterosexualized to define its true context. But it makes me sad as well.

Even though the idea of Homo Thuggism has given him a way to express himself culturally and sexually, it's also trapped him, the way it's trapped my friend Darren. Hip-hop *is* the context for many of these guys; it's the sound track of their lives, it's the basis of their politics, it's the rhythm of their rhymes. Hip-hop has given them a way to dress the part, as it were, even if they're not playing the part they're supposed to be playing. For Darren and other guys like him, being a Homo Thug means you can suck dick and yet still be perceived as powerful.

When you're wearing Timberlands as you're dicking a dude, you're fucking in context. Culturally, I suspect, it feels right. Even if you believe that everyone else thinks it's wrong.

Somewhere in the last couple of years, the American media decided that the hottest story to cover was the astonishing number of black men who have sex with black women and also with other men on the DL. From *Oprah* to the Sunday *Times Magazine,* from *Time* to *NFL Today,* the brotha on the down low is a media sensation. *On the Down Low,* a book that purports to divulge everything you need to know about life on the down low but were afraid to ask (from a formerly DLed guy's point of view), was a *New York Times* best seller. Most, if not all, of the stories are devoted to coverage of the rising rates of AIDS and HIV infections in rural and inner-city women of color. And the reason for this rise in infection rates, according to most if not all of these reports, is the suddenly shockingly large number of men living secret lives on the DL. If you've read any of the press coverage or seen any of the talk shows, black men are purportedly killing the people they love. I knew the story had reached fever pitch when Bob Costas, noted sportscaster lionized for his subtlety and intelligence, for his unsensational approach to the modern-day circus that passes for so much sporting activity, asked the correspondent who'd interviewed Roy Simmons on *NFL Today:* "Has Simmons infected anyone with the virus?"

Whoa.

How, exactly, was that any of Bob Costas's or the viewers' business? The insensitivity of the question played in my brain for days after hearing it. Partly because I was torn between wondering whether I, in fact, was being an overly sensitive black man or whether I wasn't being sensitive enough.

Yet, as we've become intimately familiar with by now, the question of where black men, particularly famous ones, put their penises has long fascinated Americans since African men were brought here as slaves. I recall a series of news articles a few years ago detailing letters Malcolm X had written to his Nation of Islam superiors about his inability to sexually fulfill Betty Shabazz. To this day, it's important for some thinkers to point out that Martin Luther King, Jr., may not have been completely faithful to Coretta Scott. Both Jesse Jackson's and Bill Cosby's "illegitimate" children have clip files as thick as my wrist. Granted these are famous men, as likely to get reported on for any number of activities in their lifetimes, but the low way in which they've been covered as sexual beings comes to mind in the wave of the DL coverage.

The cottage industry of paranoia and malice that seemed to be growing around the culture of Being On the DL feels like a return to some checkered past of black-male watching, a further race-based demonization that has historically been the black man's burden. The demonization of black men as sexual predators is not a new thing. Neither is the idea of men— of any race—leading secret sexual lives. Once upon a time, whether secret or not, it was simply called bisexuality. But there was something in this sudden burst of reportage that struck me as false and reckless. As a black man. I knew all about being studied, being poked and prodded by the powers that be, being watched and, essentially, being contained by a larger image that's needed to keep control. As my friend Lawrence said to me, "At one time, folks used a noose to hang us for how long we swing. Now we're being hung by the media for which way we swing."

The Big Finish

I wrote in *Vibe* magazine once, in a 1992 article about Sean "Puff Daddy" Combs, back when he was just an A&R guy and not a cultural phenomenon, the following: "As hip-hop makes its mad dash toward the finish line of high capitalism, it will need a hero." That hero, I hypothesized, would be Puff Daddy himself, someone so larger than life and over the top, knee-deep in the hip-hop hoopla yet fabulously fixated on the grandness of the very American dream itself, that the eventual success story that would be his life would read like a gilt-edged manual on good old American manifest destiny.

The hero, I remember thinking then, raised on *Dynasty* and *Dallas* and hip-hop's increasingly, enthusiastically craven ethos of Get Mine Now, would eventually have to out-Trump Trump, would have to out-Super Superfly.

And, through hip-hop, he has. In not just pop-culture ways, it's P. Diddy's world and we're all just living in it.

Hip-hop may have been about the black man reclaiming his masculinity from the jaws of crossover castration, about locating the crotch-grabbing hung stud in all of us, but it was also, eventually, about getting paid. Ultimately, I guess, they're the same thing: there is nothing more American than the obsessions with sex and money, with having as much as one could of both, with the ego stance of masculinity that goes along with controlling them.

I know a porn actor who thinks like a hip-hop marketing MBA and fucks, on film at least, to quote Toni Morrison from *Tar Baby,* like a star, who's hung like the proverbial horse, and is, in his industry at least, the Big Swinging Dick—the descriptive phrase Michael Lewis adapted to describe the dangerous Wall Street beast who wins at the game. I know a hip-hop marketing MBA who's hung like a porn star and fucks, to quote Toni again, like a star, from what I hear. He fancies himself a Big Swinging Dick. When I think of the ways in which black men have been defined by the hung myth—anointed with a metaphorical power that nevertheless carries some weight—it's hard for me not to think of it in terms of money. I don't know if that's because I'm a part of the get-mine generation of bling-blinging hip-hop records and ghetto superstar drug dealers and millionaire athletes for whom the 'hood will always be home or because the bling-blingers learned all they know at the feet of Blake Carrington and J. R. Ewing. I don't know if it's because when I think of the notion of the Big Swinging Dick—financially and cultur-ally—my mind goes to slavery, to the myths used for building America, to the ways in which African men were chattel, traded on the block like animals, just another product for a consumer base that didn't understand how the product was wired, so tried to reinvent it over and over again, providing the black man with a status of endowment that was as desired as it was feared.

Endowment: a funny story. I first discovered, I believe, the word "endowment" and its multiple meanings in my mid-teens, around the time I was starting to investigate colleges via the colorful brochures I found in my guidance counselor's office in school, and investigating sex via the colorful porn magazines my friends passed around. Universities were "endowed" with money, with alumni funds, and the "endowment" of a college seemed something of value and worth, something the college treated seriously. Harvard, I remember, had a huge endowment, compared to, say, Brown, the future college of my Ivy League dreams, which wasn't as well endowed as Harvard was. And, according to *Penthouse* letters I read with eagerness, men were often described as well endowed, meaning big, hung, huge. I remember giggling at the way the word could be used in such different contexts.

That was then; this is now. And the circumstances aren't all that different, are they? Harvard is, to many (and to put it in these terms) the best-hung university on the block, isn't it? It's where, to quote Margo Channing, the *"elite* meet," the crowning jewel in the tiara of America's Ivy League, where smart kids dreamed of studying alongside each other, alongside what is generally regarded as "the best and the brightest."

Like Harvard, the best endowed has access to the very best, to anything it wants, to all the things its heart desires. And, in the real world, if that's the case, it is true as well: the well-endowed man has access to the very best. And black men are the best-endowed men on the planet, right?

Ah, there's the rub. And the very twisted lie at the heart of the well-hung myth of black men. Black men have been branded with the "well-hung" label because it doesn't have to deal with the essential truth of the matter. When and where it counts, are black men really that well hung?

According to the economic civil rights group United for a Fair Economy and its study "The State of the Dream 2004" (the dream referred to being the dream in Martin Luther King, Jr.'s, famous speech), one in nine African Americans cannot find work. As reported by Renee D. Turner at BET in April of 2004: "Even with the economy producing more jobs last month than it has in four years, black unemployment continues to rise. This month's Labor Department report puts black unemployment at 10.2 percent—nearly twice that of Whites." In New York and some other major urban areas, according to labor reports, half of all black men are out of work.

"Quite frankly, there's a public policy indifference," says economist and syndicated columnist Julianne Malveaux in Turner's article. "Imagine how we would respond if we had 50 percent of white men who were unemployed. For some people it's OK for black men to be unemployed."

Florida State University economist Patrick Mason, who also presides over the National Economic Association, says, "Half of the racial difference [in unemployment figures] you can attribute to a difference in skills. The rest you have to attribute to racism."

I could roll out numbers from any and every political, social, and financial study done over the years detailing the ways in which the economic discrepancies among the races play out in the United States. I could list the studies and discussions devoted to challenging affirmative action and debating black male versus black female job opportunities and the continuing lackluster urban education. I could cite position papers and speeches and documents detailing the African American male's continued status as less than endowed on the economic, social, and political totem poles. But it almost seems to defeat the point because pop-culture-wise, black men are the cream of the crop, the definers of image, and the valued sites of desire and cultural anointment, endowed, as it were, like myths.

And maybe, eventually, that's all we have. Maybe, eventually, that will be our salvation, as America, and not just hip-hop, makes its mad dash to the finish line of high capitalism. Maybe, eventually, it is the Michael Jordans and Puff Daddys of our world who will signify what it means to be a black man, who will be the sole signposts to follow along the road to true endowment. Perhaps the myth will hold because there are men like our pop-culture and sports icons who put a face on the American dream of bigness, whether it's the real financial thing or the big-dicked-ness everyone surmises them to have. Not that Jordan and his crew are immune to adhering to some of the same mythic qualities in the American obsession. That is, if you believe journalist Sam Smith.

In his controversial book *The Jordan Rules,* averse to some swinging-dick shenanigans, Smith tells a story about Jordan and Scottie Pippen and Horace Grant, the big three of the nineties all-conquering Chicago Bulls, expressing their "hard, cutting-edge" humor styles when it came to teasing each other and teammates. Before one New York game during the 1991–92 season, Smith wrote, "Jordan, Pippen, and Grant, all of whom had boys under three at the time, had debated for a half hour about whose child had the biggest penis. They eventually agreed it was Pippen's."

Which will always remind me of a story a friend told a few years ago. My friend, let's call him Rocky, told me that he wasn't exactly the most "endowed" brother on the planet— and he blamed it on his mother. I kept my Freud jokes to myself as he recounted to me the ways in which it's the responsibility of the black mother to insure that her son be as hung as possible. And that was by pulling on her baby son's johnson, yanking on it every so often—perhaps between changes or feedings? That way it would be encouraged to grow. "You're not serious," I told Rocky.

Oh, but he was serious, serious as his dick was short. I eventually heard this dick-pulling story from other guys over the years, though I've never been bold enough to ask any of the mothers in my family whether this old wives' tale had any juice.

Rocky's story made me sad. The idea that a black man feels so cursed about his lack of dick size that he'd blame it on Mom threw me for a loop the first time I heard it. But so have so many other stories. Like the time my friend Danny met a white guy on the Internet who liked black guys, and Danny told the guy he was eight inches long, and thick.

The guy invites Danny over and they proceed to undress. As Danny gets his boxers off, the other guy—who, in Danny's description, was a BDB, or Big-Dicked Bottom— says to him, "That's not eight inches." "Uh," says Danny, "excuse me?" "That's about a seven and a half, not a true eight." Now *that*, I thought, hearing the story, is a size queen. I had a vision of the guy's apartment with a sign on the door, like at a carnival attraction, YOU MUST BE *THIS* BIG TO RIDE THIS ASS— with a ruler drawn underneath.

Turns out the guy wasn't that much of a size queen. He still had sex with Danny, whose dick, after all, is "big, black, un-cut" and, thus, "perfect" according to a guy at the sex party he'd attended.

The big black dick. I think of how many people had stories to tell me when they heard I was writing this book. I think of the white woman I met at a bar with some friends who gig-gled as she told me about her first black lover, whose penis was so big that "It was like a baby's arm!" I think of my friend's basketball coach in college who would tell the star guard on his team—who wasn't making foul shots—"You gotta put your dick on the line, man, put your big black dick on the line and just make it." Thing of it was, this particular black dude didn't have a big black dick. And everyone on the team knew it. But nothing stopped me in my tracks like the daytime TV show I saw recently.

Where have you gone Phil Donahue? Or maybe Phil would have loved this. One morning, I was watching *The View*. The guest, smack-dab in the middle of the couch, in between co-hosts Star Jones and Joy Behar, was rapper-cum-actor Snoop Doggy Dogg. He was there in that daytime hotbed of celeb estrogen to publicize his performance in the big-screen re-make of the TV show *Starsky and Hutch*. Snoop Dogg played Huggy Bear, the role originated by actor Antonio Fargas, a snitch, a street player who provides Starsky and Hutch with the information they're either too white or not hip enough to get. Huggy Bear is black. Huggy Bear is a pimp. Huggy Bear is cool. What else is new, I thought. I watched host Barbara Walters ask Snoop Dogg about his "grass" use and the porn flicks he's now producing. What else is new, I thought. But then, Star Jones asked him about a costume he didn't want to wear in the scene where he's pretending to be a golf caddy to the film's bad guy. Snoop Dogg laughs at Jones's question and even she has a mischievous glint in her eye. His laugh and her glint are because of the reason he didn't want to wear the costume, the pants in particular. They were too tight, he told the ladies and the audience and the millions of people watching at home.

They were, these pants, a "little too tight on my noodle," Snoop Dogg said, his "noodle" being a slang word for "penis" that the co-hosts had used earlier in the show.

Now *that* was new. Snoop Doggy Dogg referring to his dick on morning TV. I'd seen it all.

But maybe I'd actually seen it all on *The Oprah Winfrey Show* a few weeks prior to this episode of *The View*. On a show about the sex habits of American couples, a sex expert came on to discuss some of the sexual myths we all buy into. When she said that it, in fact, *wasn't* a myth that black men are bigger than all other men, that science has shown that black men do, indeed, on average, have the biggest dicks on the planet, the audience went positively wild, hooting and hollering, clapping and stamping, like Oprah had just tossed out one of her endless array of gifts. Was I seeing this? On TV? On *Oprah*?

I didn't know what was strangest: the mere fact of the talk of the myth, the look on Oprah's face at the audience's reaction, or the way the cameraman searched out all the black men in the crowd, particularly the ones pumping their fists in size solidarity.

Time has shown us that certain images have been shielded from our eyes because those in power didn't want us to see them. I think of Elvis Presley shaking his thing on *The Ed Sullivan Show* in the fifties, the swiveling bottom half of his body obscured from view by propriety consultants who deemed him too sexy for prime-time audiences. It's not hard to think that these guardians of cultural propriety were thinking of the female gaze in that moment, the almost Victorian way that female sexuality was denied its outlet lest society lose all sense of purpose. And it's not hard to think that these guardians were protecting whiteness from the "blackisms" Elvis had insinuated into his performing style, the raw sexuality, the powerful use of movement to make his musical points. Elvis's greasy gyrations were pre-pill, pre–women's liberation, before there was a public space for the female eye and the homosexual eye to completely redefine what the consumer gaze could withstand.

It's a long way from Elvis from the waist up to D'Angelo all over MTV, singing in a Prince-ish falsetto, his nude body spinning for all the world to see. You never see his dick, but it's implied that it's there, just below the bottom edge of your TV screen.

It's hard to point to where and when, exactly, the blatant display of black male sexuality has penetrated the public imagination. Was it Michael Jordan's tongue, as he flew through the air toward the basket, eroticizing the NBA in a way not seen in the new baggy-shorted body-hiding age?

If it wasn't Jordan, was it Dennis Rodman, who wasn't shy

about expounding on his sexual escapades, bragging about having conquered Madonna—perhaps the most famous white woman in the world, perhaps, fashionably, fabulously, the epitome of female sexual energy gone wild? He even posed nude on his book jacket, only a basketball hiding his privates. Rodman is the athlete who's threatened to strip down to nothing when he plays his final NBA game and walk off the court in all his swinging glory.

Who would have guessed that shortly after Mark Wahlberg abandoned underwear modeling for the brighter lights (and bigger-dicked parts) of Hollywood, that a brown-skinned black dude, Tyson Beckford, would become the billboard pinup star selling boxer briefs to a nation in need of support? Interestingly, Beckford's posing was done for the conservative brand Ralph Lauren, as opposed to the edgier-than-thou hipster label Calvin Klein, but perhaps that was the point. Where Calvin could maintain his status quo body-Nazi, perfect-man stance, pushing the envelope with an essentially old-thinking model, it was Ralph—who had a reputation for packaging and selling his clothes as if he was selling American nostalgia—who saw that the American public was ready to stare into the crotch of an elegantly built black dude when they opened their *New York Times Magazine* on Sunday mornings.

We've come a long way from Emmett Till.

Or have we?

"Big, as in large, as in huge . . . as in mine is better than yours."

Those are lyrics from a song called "Cadillac Car" in the Broadway musical *Dreamgirls*. It's sung by a group of brothers in the music biz who are trying to find a way to outdo the "big white man," to find a place in the pecking order of the grandiose American Dream that defines achievement and business in our culture. It's the cleverness of lyricist Tom Eyen that the song uses cars as a metaphor for "size" and success while it is set against the image of a song rising to the top of the music charts, getting bigger and bigger, as the song itself progresses the musical's storyline. Size counts, to the men in the song, the bigger the better and the bigger man always wins. Later in the musical, a character named James "Thunder" Early has an emotional breakdown onstage and strips off his clothes while singing. This action is regarded as lewd and base and ghetto and wrong by the smoother characters in the story, who are doing all they can to rise up against the "big white man" and win at his game. Early, however, wants to stay "raw," true to his own game; he doesn't want to sell out to the smooth, bland sounds of crossover.

I always found this tension in *Dreamgirls* interesting. I always found the transition from the emphasis on "size" in "Cadillac Car" to Jimmy's strip show to be one of the more honest depictions of the black male predicament in American culture, precisely because it stripped bare the ways in which black men have been forced to take sides in a debate that's always looking to define us, yet never really gives us a chance to stand at the podium and define a side for ourselves.

How often have we heard the tale of the newly rich black entertainer who goes out and buys a big car before anything else? How often have we heard the tale of the white label owner who buys a car to satisfy the jones of the black talent he has no intention of paying his full financial due? What is hip-hop, if not James "Thunder" Early's stripping down to raw basics to take back the black man's share of the game's constantly rewritten rules?

Entertainment has been used so often as a site to talk about the issues in this book because entertainment is the place where black folks have been allowed *some* semblance of power in American culture. The tropes of movie characters and TV comics and recording stars have defined so much American behavior it would be easy to think that the description of mass media as a form of mass hypnosis makes more and more sense to me as I get older. And as I get older, I'm struck more and more by the ways in which, even as more and more blacks take on leadership positions in corporate America—joining Stewart's "Big Swinging Dicks" at the boardroom tables—it's the popular arts (and sports) that continue to dominate the mass imagination as a way of defining black people.

And I include black people as part of that mass imagination.

I have a black friend who fooled around with a largely endowed black dude; my friend nicknamed the guy Amistad because the guy resembled actor Djimon Hounsou. That name always struck me as odd—Amistad was the name of a boat bringing slaves to the New World upon which the slaves revolted en route. But my friend was using "Amistad" as if it was the name of one of the slaves—like the way people use the word Mandingo. When my friend used this name, I flashed back on how Mandingo is a slave name used to describe a certain kind of black man or a certain kind of behav-ior—all based on a misreading of the real Mandingo story. Have black folks become as guilty of hanging on to the same stereotypes that have defined the community since it became part of the New World? Are we as culpable for our stereo-types as the white folks we blame them on? No brother is mad at being considered a heavy-dicked sex machine; in fact, we've all sung along with James Brown when the song blasted from any nearby speaker. But what do we gain from it? We need to start thinking like the Big Swinging Dicks on Wall Street instead of acting like the Big Swinging Dicks of the public's fascination. And until a wholesale think-state changes to believe that, we'll be recording records instead of truly owning them.

Epilogue

Dear Emmett Till—

Black men are still singing the blues. We get richer doing it these days, even though we've relinquished the low-slung guitar to our white brethren and taken up a different kind of phallic representation—the microphone—to showcase our sound. We even get to shout out words like *nigger* and *pussy* and *bitch* from stages around the globe. Can you imagine that?

There was this group back in the late eighties and early nineties called 2 Live Crew. They had a big hit with the song called "Me So Horney." They "rapped" some nasty rhymes and got threatened with the long hand of the law because their work was deemed "obscene" by common American standards of decency. I wish you could have seen it, Emmett. It was like the "Negro Problem" all over again. The debate surrounding the "decency" of this music reached almost ecstatic levels, reaching a crescendo when it was decided that records like those by 2 Live Crew would be "stickered"—marked, as it were—by the sign of the government's desire to keep those randy sorts who'd make life unsafe for everyone else under control.

You know something about that.

Sometimes I have to laugh, Emmett, as I watch my people struggle with their status in this place we call home. Sometimes I have to laugh at the cartoonish ways we have of showcasing what we think of as our most powerful selves, *trying* to build some kind of legacy that will cut through the daunting and overreaching tyranny of "American masculinity" that has dogged black men since we got here.

But perhaps you will have the last laugh. Perhaps we all will, however morbid that might sound. Because you are in the news again, Emmett, as I write the words that fill this book. Black men who've felt as haunted by you as I have been have started to recover your dignity, to seek out once again the men who snuffed out your vigorous youth with the power of racism.

Some things have changed. We've become more a part of the national debate rather than just being the subject of the national debate. And maybe we aren't letting white folks into our heads as much. Because, unlike you, that's what we'd all done at some point in our lives. Let white folks get into our heads. White folks like the white chick from RISD Tap Room who introduced me to my own sense of my mythical self. I think of the impetus for Latin boy Nico to adopt his black boy mask. And then there's Simon, with his towels wound tightly around him, hiding himself, discreet to the point of dehumanizing himself. I feel sad for him, yet I understand. Dude just wants to be a man. Like you did.

> Watching, living, and waiting,
> Your boy,
> Scott